The Diary
AND
OBSERVATIONS
OF
THOMAS ALVA EDISON

EDISON IN HIS CHEMICAL LABORATORY

The Diary
AND
OBSERVATIONS
OF
THOMAS ALVA EDISON

**EDITED BY
DAGOBERT D. RUNES**

A Philosophical Paperback

Philosophical Library
New York

ACKNOWLEDGMENTS

The publishers are indebted to the following for permission to reprint selections from their publications:

New York Times, Springfield (Mass.) News, New York American, New York World, The Mentor, The (Newark) Sunday Call, The Forum, Strand Magazine, The (Dearborn) Independent, American Magazine, Socony Standard, New York Herald, Scientific American, The Princetonian, Collier's, New York Journal, McClure's, Musical Monitor, Musical America, Cosmopolitan, Hearst's International, Baltimore (Md.) American, New York Mail, American Scrapbook.

The editor wishes to thank Mr. Norman R. Speiden, curator of the Thomas Alva Edison Foundation, West Orange, New Jersey, for his kind assistance in the preparation of this volume.

ISBN 8022-2434-2

Copyright 1948, 1976 by Philosophical Library, Inc., 200 West 57th Street, New York, N.Y. 10019. Printed in the United States of America.

The numerals appearing at the foot of each excerpt indicate the date of the respective paper or talk.

CONTENTS

Part One

	PAGE
THE DIARY	1

Part Two

	PAGE
SUNDRY OBSERVATIONS	39

CHAPTER		PAGE
I	AUTOBIOGRAPHICAL	43
II	MOTION PICTURES AND THE ARTS	61
	Money and movies	63
	The beginning of motion pictures	68
	On music	79
	Our musical future	84
III	WAR AND PEACE	89
	On atomic energy	91
	Chances of war	92
	Harnessing of new powers	93
	The wars of tomorrow	94
	On disarmament conferences	95
	The fight against radicalism	99
IV	EDUCATION AND WORK	105
	Education and speed	107
	Obsolete education	111
	Memory testing	114

			PAGE
		The habit of forgetting	118
		The new generation	120
		The unrest of youth	122
		Maturity and youth	123
		Employment and education	128
		The will to work	140
		The college of business	141
		Visual education	145
CHAPTER			
V	THE PHILOSOPHY OF PAINE		149
VI	MAN AND MACHINE		159
		They won't think	166
		Machine and progress	171
		They do what they like to do	178
		The inventor's lot	179
		The desire for change	179
		Age and achievement	180
VII	FOR A BETTER WORLD		183
		Economics of fear	185
		The standard of gold	192
		Nations and the gold standard	195
VIII	THE REALMS BEYOND		203
		Life after death	205
		Life's flashbacks	209
		Memory units	215
		The mystery of life	216
		Spiritualism	232
		Spirit communication	238
	INDEX		245

PREFACE

FEW MEN have contributed more to the well-being and comfort of modern man than Thomas Alva Edison. The glow of the electric light, and with it the waves of immortal music come right into the homes of the world's great masses, through the inventive genius of this unassuming tinkerer; and through his efforts the theatre on the screen reaches into every hamlet on the globe.

With his more than one thousand inventions, Edison symbolizes the inauguration of the electro-industrial era of our time.

Edison was almost Franklinian in his defiance of the doctrines of pure science. He was an experimenter and a practical man more than an ingenious theoretician. His inventions were the product of a methodical and prodding mind. There were no sudden flashes of accidental discovery in his realm.

His book knowledge was scattered, sporadic and unsystematic; he was almost entirely self-educated. He would read the *Police Gazette* one hour and the *Journal of Higher Mathematics* the next. A man of the people, working for a living and for his "experimental equipment," from the age of twelve on his mind was perennially active for the people and their welfare. He was, without doubt, in the words of Marconi, "one of the world's greatest benefactors."

The editor has endeavored, in this volume, to present to the reader a selection of Edison's social and philosophic ideas taken from the available notes, statements and observations of the inventor. The reader will find that many of Edison's casual remarks made decades ago have a definite contemporary significance. His propositions in ethics, philosophy, music and education show a rare combination of whimsey and deep sincerity.

D. D. R.

The Diary

Menlo Park, N. J.
Sunday, July 12, 1885

Awakened at 5:15 A.M. My eyes were embarrassed by the sunbeams—turned my back to them and tried to take another dip into oblivion—succeeded—awakened at 7 A.M. Thought of Mina,* Daisy, and Mamma G—. Put all 3 in my mental kaleidoscope to obtain a new combination à la Galton. Took Mina as a basis, tried to improve her beauty by discarding and adding certain features borrowed from Daisy and Mamma G. A sort of Raphaelized beauty, got into it too deep, mind flew away and I went to sleep again.

Awakened at 8:15 A.M. Powerful itching of my head, lots of white dry dandruff—what is this d—mnable material. Perhaps it's the dust from the dry literary matter I've crowded into my noodle lately. Its nomadic. Gets all over my coat; must read about it in the Encyclopedia.

Smoking too much makes me nervous—must lasso

* Mina Miller, daughter of Lewis Miller of Akron, Ohio. She and Mr. Edison were married Feb. 24, 1886.
   Mamma G. was wife of Ezra Gilliland (nicknamed Damon), who was Edison's friend from his days as telegrapher and was at this time working with him on a form of wireless telegraph.

my natural tendency to acquire such habits—holding heavy cigar constantly in my mouth has deformed my upper lip, it has a sort of Havana curl.

Arose at 9 o'clock; came downstairs expecting 'twas too late for breakfast—'twasn't. Couldn't eat much, nerves of stomach too nicotinny. The root of tobacco plants must go clear through to hell. Satan's principal agent Dyspepsia must have charge of this branch of the vegetable kingdom. It has just occured to me that the brain may digest certain portions of food, say the etherial part, as well as the stomach—perhaps dandruff is the excreta of the mind—the quantity of this material being directly proportional to the amount of reading one indulges in.

A book on German metaphysics would thus easily ruin a dress suit. After breakfast started reading Hawthorne's English Note Book, don't think much of it—perhaps I'm a literary barbarian and am not yet educated up to the point of appreciating fine writing—90 per cent of his book is descriptive of old churches and graveyards and coronors. He and Geo. Selwyn ought to have been appointed perpetual coroners of London.

Two fine things in the book were these: Hawthorne showing to little Rose Hawthorne * a big live lobster, told her it was a very ugly thing and would bite

* Rose Hawthorne married George Parsons Lathrop, with whom Edison started to collaborate on a "Jules Verne" type of inventive prophecy. He therefore was well acquainted with her a few years after this diary was written.

everybody, whereupon she asked, "if the first one God made bit him—" Again

"Ghostland is beyond the jurisdiction of veracity" —I think freckles on the skin are due to some salt of Iron, sunlight brings them out by reducing them from high to low state of oxidation—perhaps with a powerful magnet applied for some time, and then with proper chemicals, these mud holes of beauty might be removed.

Dot * is very busy cleaning the abode of our deaf and dumb parrot—she has fed it tons of edibles, and never got a sound out of it. This bird has the taciturnity of a statue, and the dirt producing capacity of a drove of buffalo.

This is by far the nicest day of this season, neither too hot nor too cold—it blooms on the apex of perfection—an Edenday. Good day for an angels' picnic. They could lunch on the smell of flowers and new mown hay, drink the moisture of the air, and dance to the hum of bees. Fancy the soul of Plato astride of a butterfly riding around Menlo Park with a lunch basket.

Nature is bound to smile somehow. Holzer † has a little dog which just came on the veranda. The face of this dog was as dismal as a bust of Dante, but the

---

* Dot was the nickname of Edison's oldest daughter, Marion Edison, then 12 years old.

† Wm. Holzer, one of Edison's Menlo Park associates who, having married Alice Stilwell (sister of Edison's first wife), was living in the old Edison home at Menlo Park.

dog wagged its tail continuously. This is evidently the way a dog laughs. I wonder if dogs ever go up to flowers and smell them—I think not—flowers were never intended for dogs and perhaps only incidentally for man. Evidently Darwin has it right. They make themselves pretty to attract the insect world who are the transportation agents of their pollen—pollen freight via Bee line.

There is a bumblebee's nest somewhere near this veranda. Several times one came near me. Some little information (acquired experimentally) I obtained when a small boy causes me to lose all delight in watching the navigation of this armed flower burglar.

Had dinner at 3 P.M. Ruins of a chicken, rice pudding. I eat too quick. At 4 o'clock Dot came around with her horse "Colonel" and took me out riding—beautiful roads—saw 10 acre lot full of cultivated red raspberries. "A burying ground" so to speak. Got this execrable pun off on Dot.

Dot says she is going to write a novel, already started on. She has the judgment of a girl of 16, although only 12.

We passed through the town of Metuchen. This town was named after an Indian chief. They called him Metuchen, the chief of the rolling lands, the country being undulating. Dot laughed heartily when I told her about a church being a heavenly fire-escape.

Returned from drive at 5 P.M. Commenced reading short sketches of life's Macauley, Sidney Smith, Dickens and Charlotte Bronte. Macauley, when only 4 years old, omnivorous reader; used book language in his childish conversation. When 5 years old, lady spilled some hot coffee on his legs. After a while she asked him if he was better. He replied, "Madam, the agony has abated." Macauley's mother must have built his mind several years before his body.

Sidney Smith's flashes of wit are perfect—to call them chestnuts would be literary blasphemy. They are wandering jewelets to wander forever in the printers' world. Don't like Dickens—don't know why. I'll stock my literary cellar with his works later.

Charlotte Bronte was like DeQuincy. What a nice married couple they would have been. I must read Jane Eyre. Played a little on the piano; it's badly out of tune. Two keys have lost their voice.

Dot just read to me outlines of her proposed novel. The basis seems to be a marriage under duress. I told her that in case of a marriage to put in bucketfuls of misery. This would make it realistic. Speaking of realism in painting, etc., Steele Mackaye, at a dinner given to H. H. Porter, Wm. Winter and myself, told us of a definition of modern realism given by some Frenchman whose name I have forgotten. "Realism is a dirty long-haired painter sitting on the head of a bust of Shakespeare painting a pair of old boots covered with dung."

The bell rings for supper. Igoe sardines the principal attraction. On seeing them was attacked by a stroke of vivid memory of some sardines I ate last winter that caused a rebellion in the labyrinth of my stomach. Could scarcely swallow them today. They nearly did the "return ball" act.

After supper Dot pitched a ball to me several dozen times—first I ever tried to catch. It was as hard as Nero's heart—nearly broke my baby-finger. Gave it up. Taught Dot and Maggie how to play "Duck on the rock." They both thought it great fun. And this is Sunday. My conscience seems to be oblivious of Sunday. It must be incrusted with a sort of irreligious tartr. If I was not so deaf I might go to church and get it taken off or at least loosened. Eccavi! I will read the new version of the bible.

Holzer is going to use the old laboratory for the purpose of hatching chickens artificially by an electric incubator. He is very enthusiastic. Gave me full details. He is a very patient and careful experimenter. Think he will succeed. Everything succeeded in that old laboratory.

Just think electricity employed to cheat a poor hen out of the pleasures of maternity. Machine-born chickens! What is home without a mother?

I suggested to H that he vaccinate his hens with chicken-pox virus. Then the eggs would have their embryo hereditarily inoculated and none of the chickens would have the disease. For economy's sake he could start with one hen and rooster. He being a scientific man with no farm experience, I explained the necessity of having a rooster. He saw the force of this suggestion at once.

The sun has left us on time. Am going to read from the Encyclopedia Brittanica to steady my nerves, and go to bed early. I will shut my eyes and imagine a terraced abyss, each terrace occupied by a beautiful maiden. To the first I will deliver my mind and they will pass it down to the uttermost depths of silence and oblivion. Went to bed. Worked my imagination for a supply of maidens. Only saw Mina, Daisy and Mamma. Scheme busted—sleep.

Menlo Park, N. J.
July 13, 1885

Woke (is there such a word?) at 6 o'clock. Slipped down the declivity of unconsciousness again until 7. Arose and tried to shave with a razor so dull that every time I scraped my face it looked as if I was in the throes of cholera morbus. By shaving often I, to a certain extent, circumvent the diabolical malignity of these razors. If I could get my mind down to details perhaps could learn to sharpen it, but on the other hand I might cut myself.

As I had to catch the 7.30 A.M. train for New York, I hurried breakfast, crowded meat, potatoes, eggs, coffee, tandem down into the chemical room of my body. I've now got dyspepsia in that diabolical thing that Carlyle calls the stomach. Rushed and caught train. Bought a New York *World* at Elizabeth for my mental breakfast. Among the million of perfected mortals on Manhattan Island two of them took it into their heads to cut their navel cord from mother earth and be born into a new world, while two other less developed citizens stopped two of their neighbors from living. The details of these two little incidents conveyed to my mind what beautiful creatures we live among and how, with the aid of the police, civilization so rapidly advances.

Went to New York via Desbrosses Street ferry.

Tooks cars across town. Saw a woman get into car that was so tall and frightfully thin as well as dried up that my mechanical mind at once conceived the idea that it would be the proper thing to run a lancet into her arm and knee joints and insert automatic self-feeding oil cups to diminish the creaking when she walked.

Got off at Broadway. Tried experiment of walking two miles to our office—65 Fifth Avenue *—with idea it would alleviate my dsypeptic pains. It didn't.

Went into Scribner & Sons on way up, saw about a thousand books I wanted. Right off Mind No. 1 said, Why not buy a box full and send to Boston now. Mind No. 2 (acquired and worldly mind) gave a most withering mental glance at Mind No. 1 and said, You fool, buy only two books. These you can carry without trouble and will last until you get to Boston. Buying books in New York to send to Boston is like "carrying coals to Newcastle." Of course I took the advice of this earthly adviser. Bought Aldrich's story of a bad boy, which is a spongecake kind of literature, very witty and charming, and a work on Goethe and Schiller by Boynsen, which is soggy literature. A little wit and anecdote in this style of literature would have the same effect as baking soda on bread—give pleasing results.

Waited one hour for the appearance of a lawyer who is to cross-examine me on events that occurred

* Office of the Edison Electric Light Company.

eleven years ago. Went on stand at 11.30. He handed me a piece of paper with some figures on it, not another mark. Asked in a childlike voice if these were my figures, what they were about and what day eleven years ago I made them. This implied compliment to the splendor of my memory was at first so pleasing to my vanity that I tried every means to trap my memory into stating just what he wanted—but then I thought what good is a compliment from a ten-cent lawyer, and I waived back my recollection. A lawsuit is the suicide of time.

Got through at 3.30 P.M. Waded through a lot of accumulated correspondence mostly relating to other people's business. Insull saw Wiman about getting car for Railroad Telegh experiment. Will get costs in day or so. Tomlinson made Sammy mad by saying he (Insull) was valet to my intellect. Got $100. Met Dot and skipped for the Argosy of the Puritan Sea, i.e., Sound Steamboat. Dot is reading a novel—rather trashy. Love hash. I completed reading Aldrich's Bad Boy and advanced fifty pages in Goethe, then retired to a "Sound" sleep.

Woodside Villa
July 14, 1885

Dot introduced me to a new day at 5.30 A.M. Arose, toileted quickly, breakfasted, then went from boat to street car. Asked colored gentleman how long before car left. Worked his articulating apparatus so weakly I didn't hear word he said. It's nice to be a little deaf when traveling. You can ask everybody directions, then pump your imagination for the answer. It strengthens this faculty.

Took train leaving at 7 from Providence for the metropolis of culture. Arrived there 9 A.M. "Coupaid" it to Damon's office. Waited three-quarters hour for his arrival, then left for the Chateau-sur-le-Mer. If I stay there much longer Mrs. G—— will think me a bore. Perhaps she thinks I make only two visits each year in one place each of six months. Noticed there was no stewardess on the ferryboat. Strange omission considering the length of the voyage and the swell made by the tri-monthly boat to Nantucket. Man with a dusty railroad company expression let down a sort of portcullis and the passengers poured themselves out.

Arrived Winthrop Junction, found Patrick there according to telephone instruction, another evidence that the telephone works sometimes. Patrick had the Americanized dog cart and incidentally a horse. Suppose Patrick would have forgotten the horse, because last week he went into Boston to Damon's city residence and turned on the gas and started up the motor from a state of innocence to the wildest prevarication and forgot to turn gas off.

Arrived at Woodside Villa and was greeted by Mamma with a smile as sweet as a cherub that buzzed around the bedside of Raphael. A fresh invoice of innocence and beauty had arrived in my absence in the persons of Miss Louise Igoe,* and her aunt, like Miss Daisy, is from Indianapolis, that producer of Hoosier Venuses. Miss Igoe is a pronounced blonde, blue eyes, with a complexion as clear as the conscience of a baby angel, with hair like Andromache. Miss Igoe's aunt is a bright elderly lady who beat me so bad at checkers that my bump of "Strategic combination" has sunk in about two inches.

For fear that Mrs. G—— might think I had an inexhaustible supply of dirty shirts, I put on one of those starched horrors procured for me by Tomlinson. Put my spongy mind at work on life Goethe. Chewed some Tulu gum presented me by Mrs. G——. Conceived the idea that the mastication of this chunk of illimitable plasticity—a dentiferous tread-mill so to speak—would act on the salivial glands to produce an excess of this necessary ingredient of the digestive fluid and thus a self-acting home-made remedy for

---

* Louise Igoe married Robert Anderson Miller, brother of Mina Miller.

dyspepsia would be obtained. Believe there is something in this as my dyspeptic pains are receding from recognition.

Dot is learning to play Lange's "Blumenlied" on the piano. Miss Igoe, I learn from a desultory conversation, is involved in a correspondence with a brother of Miss Mina, who resides at Canton, Ohio, being connected with the mower and reaper firm of Aultman J. Miller. The letter received today being about as long as the bills at the Grand Hotel at Paris are, I surmise, of rather a serious character, cupidly speaking. The frequency of their reception will confirm or disaffirm my conjectures as to the proximity of a serious catastrophe. A postoffice courtship is a novelty to me, so I have resolved to follow up this matter for the experience which I will obtain. This may come handy should "my head ever become the dupe of my heart" as papa Rochefoucauld puts it.

In evening went out on sea wall. Noticed a strange phosphorescent light in the west, probably caused by a baby moon just going down Chinaward. Thought at first the Aurora Borealis had moved out west. Went to bed early, dreamed of a Demon with eyes four hundred feet apart.

Woodside Villa
July 15, 1885

Slept well. Breakfasted clear up to my adam's apple. Took shawl strap and went to Boston with Damon with following memorandum of things to get.

Lavater on the human face, Miss Cleveland's book, Heloise by Rosseau, short neckties, Wilhelm Meister, basket fruit, Sorrows of Werther, Madame Recamier's works, Diary books, pencils, telephone documents, Mark Twain's gummed Potentiality of Literature, i.e., scrap book. Also book called "How Success Is Won," containing life of Dr. Vincent and something in it about Mina's father and your humble servitor.

Found that only copy of Lavater which I saw the other day had been sold to some one who was on the same lay as myself. Bought Disraeli's Curiosities of Literature instead. Got Miss C's book, Twain's scrap book, diary books, How Success Is Won, also fruit, among which are some peaches which the vendor said came from California. Think of a lie three thousand miles long. There seemed to be a South Carolina accent in their taste.

Started back to office with fruit, apparently by the same route I came. Brought up in a strange street. Saw landmark and got on right course again. Boston ought to be buoyed and charts furnished strangers.

Damon suggests American District Messenger buoys with uniform.

Saw a lady who looked like Mina. Got thinking about Mina and came near being run over by a street car. If Mina interferes much more will have to take out an accident policy.

Went to dinner at a sort of no-bread-with-one-fishball restaurant, then came up towards Damon's office. Met Damon, Madden and Ex-Governor Howard of Rhode Island. The Governor, whom I knew and who is very deaf, greeted me with a boiler-yard voice. He has to raise his voice so he can hear himself to enable him to check off the accuracy of his pronunciation. The Governor never has much time, always in a hurry—full of business, inebriated with industry. If he should be on his death bed I believe he would call in a shorthand clerk to dictate directions for his funeral, short sketch of his life, taking a press copy of the same in case of litigation.

Madden looks well in the face, but I am told it's an undertakers' blush. Went to Damon's office. He was telling me about a man who had a genius for stupidity when Vail came in dressed like Beau Brummel. Both went into another room to try some experiments on Damon's Phonometer.

Saw Hovey, a very, very bright newspaper man. Told me a story related to him by a man who I never would have imagined could or would have told such stories. I refer to a gentleman in the employment of the telephone company whom Tomlinson nicknamed "Prepositum" because he got off that word in a business conversation. His eminent respectability so impressed Tomlinson that when he came out of his office he asked me to take him quickly somewhere disreputable so he could recover. This story would have embarrassed Satan. I shall not relate it, but I have called it "Prepositum's Turkish Compromise." Hovey told me a lot about a sixth sense, mind reading, etc. Made some suggestions about Railroad Telegraph.

Came home with Damon at 5 o'clock. Damon has an ulcerated molar.

Just before supper Mrs. Roberts and another lady came in to visit Mrs. G. Mrs. R. is a charming woman —condensed sunshine—beautiful—plays piano like a long-haired professor. Played several of Lange's pieces first time seeing them. This seems as incomprehensible to me as a man reciting the Lord's Prayer in four languages simultaneously. Mrs. R. promised to come tomorrow evening and bring with her a lady who sings beautifully and a boy dripping with music.

Everyone after supper started their Diary. Mrs. G., Igoe, Daisy and Dot went to bed at 11.30. Forgot two nights running to ask Damon for night shirt. That part of my memory which has charge of the night shirt department is evidently out of order.

Woodside Villa
July 16, 1885

I find on waking up this morning that I went to bed last night with the curtains up in my room. Glad the family next door retire early. I blushed retroactively to think of it. Slept well. Weather clear, warm. Thermometer prolangatively progressive. Day so fine that barometer anaethized. Breakfasted. Diaried a lot of nonsense. Read some of Longfellow's Hyperion, read to where he tells about a statue of a saint that was attacked with somnambulism and went around nights with a lantern repairing roofs, especially that of a widow woman who neglected her family to pray all day in the church.

Read account of two murders in morning *Herald* to keep up my interest in human affairs. Built an air castle or two. Took my new shoes out on a trial trip. Read some of Miss Cleveland's book where she goes for George Eliot for not having a heavenly streak of imaginative twaddle in her poetry. The girls assisted by myself trimmed the Elizabeth collars on twelve daisies, inked eyes, nose and mouth on the yellow part which gave them a quaint human look. Paper dresses were put on them, and all were mounted on the side of a paper box and labeled "The Twelve Daughters of Venus." I hope no college-bred dude will come down here and throw out insinuations that Venus was never married and never had any children anyway.

Girls went in bathing. Damon and I went out in the steam yacht, sailed around over the lobster nursery for an hour or so. In the evening Damon started a diary—very witty. Miss Igoe told Damon she couldn't express her admiration, whereupon he told her to send it by freight. Lunched our souls on a Strauss waltz played by Miss Daisy, then we all sat around the table to write up our diaries. I taught the girls how to make shadow pictures by use of crumpled paper. We tried some experiments in mind reading which were not very successful. Think mind reading contrary to common sense, wise provision of the Bon Dieu that we cannot read each other's minds. 'Twould stop civilization and everybody would take to the woods. In fifty or a hundred thousand centuries, when mankind has become perfect by evolution, then perhaps this sense could be developed with safety to the state. Damon and I went into a minute expense account of our proposed earthly paradise in the land of flowers, also a duplicate north and we concluded to take short views of life and go ahead with the scheme. It will make a savage onslaught on our bank account. Damon remarked that now all the wind work is done there only remains some little details to attend to, such as "raising the money," etc. Mrs. Roberts hurt her Soprano arm and could not come over and play for us as promised, and thus we lost her perfumed conversation, lovely music and seraphic smile. *La-femme qui-rit.* Since Miss Igoe has been reading Miss Cleveland's book her language has become dissyllabic, ponderous, stiff and formal, each observation seems laundered.

If this weather gets much hotter, Hell will get up a reputation as a summer resort. Dot asked how books went in the mail. Damon said as second class mail matter. I said Damon and I would go at this rating —suggested that Mina would have to pay full postage. Damon thought she should be registered. This reminds me that I read the other day of a man who applied for a situation as sexton in the dead letter office. Daisie's sister's photograph rests on the mantel, shows very beautiful girl. Every fly that has attempted to light on it has slipped and fallen. Going to put piece of chalk near it so they can chalk their feet. This will permit with safety the insectiverous branch of nature to gaze upon a picture of what they will attain after ages of evolution. Ladies went to bed. This removed the articutating upholstery. Then we went to bed.

Woodside Villa
July 17, 1885

Slept so sound that even Mina didn't bother me, as it would stagger the mind of Raphael in a dream to imagine a being comparable to the Maid of Chautaqua, so I must have slept very sound. As usual I was the last one up. This is because I'm so deaf. Found everybody smiling and happy. Read more of Miss Cleveland's book. Think she is a smart woman—relatively. Damon's diary progressing finely. Patrick went to city to get tickets for opera of Polly. We can com*parrot* with Sullivan's.

We are going out with the ladies in yacht to sail, perchance to fish. The lines will be baited at both end. Constantly talking about Mina, whom Damon and I use as a sort of yardstick for measuring perfection. Makes Dot jealous. She threatens to become an incipient Lucretia Borgia.

Hottest day of season. Hell must have sprung a leak. At two o'clock went out on yacht—cooler on the water. Sailed out to the Rock-buoy. This is the point where Damon goes to change his mind. He circles the boat around several times like a carrier pigeon before starting out on a journey. Then we start right. Dropped anchor in a shady part of the open bay. I acted as master of the fish lines, delivered them baited to all. The clam coquets were thrown to the piscatorial actors. Miss Daisy caught the first. He came up smilingly to seize the bouquet when she jerked him into the dress circle, genus unknown. I caught the next—genus uncertain. The next was not caught.

Fish seem to be rather conservative around this bay. One seldom catches enough to form the fundamental basis for a lie. Dante left out one of the torments of Hades. I could imagine a doomed mortal made to untangle wet fish lines forever. Everybody lost patience at the stupidity of the fish in not coming forward promptly to be murdered. We hauled up anchor, and Damon, steering by the compass (he being by it), made for the vicinity of Apple Island. While approaching it we saw a race between two little model vessels, full rigged and about two feet long. Two yawl boats, filled apparently with U. S. naval officers and men, were following them. Are these effeminate pursuits a precursor of the decline and fall of a country as history tells us?

Landed at dock 4:30. Came into villa and commenced reading Lavater on Facial Philosophy. Dot saw a jellyfish and vehemently called our attention to this translucent chestnut. Barge called to take us to theatre via Winthrop Junction and railroad. When we arrived at Junction found we should have to wait some time, so we took an open street car for city. While passing along saw man on bicycle, asked Damon if he ever rode one. He said he did, once practiced riding in large freight shed where floor was even with door of cars and three feet from ground. One day, for reason he never could explain, he went right through one of the doors to the ground. I remarked that I supposed he kept right on riding. No, said Damon, I jumped back.

Arriving at ferryboat I asked Damon if it was further across river at high tide. Said he thought it was as he noticed the piles in the slip were at a slight angle.

Arriving on the other side, took street gondola. Arrived near top of Hanover Street. When horses were unable to pull cars to the top of the hill, car slipped back. The executive department of my body was about to issue a writ of ejectment when some of the passengers jumped out and stopped car. One passenger halloed out to let her go, they would get more ride.

Arriving a little too early for theatre, went to an ice cream bazaar, frigidified ourselves. Then went to theatre, where we found it very hot. Solomon the composer came from the cellar of fairies and sprung a chestnut overture on the few mortals in the audience chamber. Then the curtain arose showing the usual number of servant girls in tights. The raising of the panoply of fairyland let some more heat in—a rushing sound was heard and Damon said they were turning off the steam. The fairies mopped their foreheads. Perspiration dripped down on stage from the painted cherub over the arch. After numerous military evolutions by the chorus Miss Lillian Russell made her appearance. Beautiful woman, sweet voice. Wore a fur-lined cloak which I thought about as appropriate in this weather as to clothe the firemen on the Red Sea steamers in sealskin overcoats. Noticed one or two original strains. The balance of the music seemed to be Bagpipean Improvastarationes. Didn't hear anything that was spoken except once when I thought I heard one of the actors say that his mother sang in the Chinese ballet. Our seats were in the bald-head section.

After theatre walked to ferryboat. Saw a steamer passing brilliantly lighted. Mrs. G. asked what could be nicer than a lighted steamer on the waters at night. Somebody suggested two steamers. Arrived at sister ferry, took railroad train, saw Miss Russell with her last husband, Mr. Solomon, get on train. They stop, I believe, at the sea shore near us. Home—Bed—Sleep.

Woodside
July 18, 1885

Last night room was very close, single sheet over me seemed inch thick. Bug-proof windows seems to repel obtrusiveness on the part of any prowling zephyr that might want to come in and lunch on perspiration. Rolled like a ship in a typhoon. If this weather keeps on I'll wear holes in the bedclothes.

Arose early. Weather blasphemingly hot. Went out in sun. Came back dripping with water. Tried to get into the umbrella rack to drain off. Took off two courses of clothes. This would be good day to adopt Sidney Smith's plan of taking off your flesh and sitting down in your bones. Memo—go to a print cloth mill and have yourself run through the calico printing machine. This would be the Ultima Thule of thin clothing.

Read some in Lavater, Wm. Recamier, Rousseau's Émile. Laid down on sofa, fell asleep. Dreamed that Damon had the sunstroke and was laid on the floor of his office, where he swelled up so that he broke the floor above and two editors of a baseball journal fell through and were killed. Thought the chief of the fire department came in and ordered holes to be bored in him. Then something changed the dream. Saw a lot of animals with such marvelous characteristics as would be sufficient to bust up the whole science of paleontology. Cuvier and Darwin never could have started their theories had a few samples of these animals ever browsed around on this little mud ball of ours. After a survey of this vast imaginative menagerie I woke up by nearly falling off the sofa. Found the heat had reached the apex of its malignity.

Went out yachting, all the ladies in attendance. I was delightfully unhot. Ladies played game called memory-scheme. No. 1 calls out name of prominent author, No. 2 repeats this name and adds another and so on. Soon one has to remember a dozen names, all of which must be repeated in the order given. Result, Miss Daisy had the best and I the poorest memory. We played another game called "pon honor," resultant of which is that if you are caught you must truthfully answer a question put by each player. These questions generally relate to the amours of the players.

Arrived home at 7:30. Yacht brought in too far and left stranded by the receding of the tide. Suppered, went out and saw some fireworks set off by an unknown sojourner in these ozonic parts. Afterwards went over to Cottage Park at the kind invitation of the charming Mrs. Roberts to hear the band play pro bono publico and her boy exclusivemento. Boy is quite a prodigy on the piano, plays with great rapidity. His hands and fingers went like a buzzsaw Played a solemn piece which I imagined might be

God Kill the Queen. In walking back Miss Igoe got several boulders in her shoes. Miss Daisy smiled so sweetly all the evening that I imagined a ray of sunshine tried to pass her and got stuck. Mrs. Roberts caught cold in her arm. Its cough is better. Home—bed—oblivion.

Woodside Villa
July 19, 1885

Slept as sound as a bug in a barrel of morphine. Donned a boiled and starched emblem of respectability. Ate food for breakfast. Weather delightful. Canary seed orchestra started up with same old tune. Ancestors of this bird sang the selfsame tune six thousand years ago to Adam down on the Euphrates, way back when Abel got a situation as the first angel.

Read Sunday *Herald,* learned of John Roche's failure. Am sorry. He has been pursued with great malignity by newspapers and others, from ignorance I think. Americans ought to be proud of Roche, who started in life as a day laborer and became the giant of industry and the greatest shipbuilder in the United States, employing thousands of men and feeding innumerable families. What has he now for this forty years of incessant work and worry? For people who hound such men as these I would invent a special Hades. I would stricken them with the chronic sciatic neuralgia and cause them to wander forever stark naked within the arctic circle. Saw in some paper account of baseball match. This struck me as something unusual. Read more about that immeasurable immensity of tact and beauty Madame Recamier. I would like to see such a woman. Nature seems to be running her factory on another style of goods nowadays and won't switch back until long after I'm bald-headed.

Damon went out to assist the tide in. Daisy told me something about a man who kept a livery stable in Venice. In afternoon went out in yacht. On first trip all our folks and lot of smaller people sailed around for an hour, returned and landed the abbreviated people. Started for Cottage Park, where we took on board the charming Mrs. Robert, brévet Recamier, and a large lady friend whose name has twice got up and jumped out of my mind. Then sailed away for Rock-buoy and for some occult reason Damon didn't stop and change his mind, but headed for Liverpool. Went out two miles in ocean. Undulations threatened to disturb the stability of the dinner of divers persons. Returned at 7 P.M. Then Damon took out a boatload of slaves of the kitchen.

Damon and I, after his return, study plans for our Floridian bower in the lowlands of the peninsular Eden, within that charmed zone of beauty, where wafted from the table lands of the Oronoco and the dark Carib Sea, perfumed zephyrs forever kiss the gorgeous flora. Rats! Damon took the plans to Boston to place them into the hands of an architect to be reduced to a paper reality. Damon promised to ascertain probable cost chartering schooner to plough the Spanish main loaded with our hen coops.* Dot

* Edison's home and laboratory at Fort Myers, Florida, was shipped from Maine.

came in and gave us a lot of girlish philosophy which amused us greatly. Oh dear, this celestial mud ball has made another revolution and no photograph yet received from the Chataquain Paragon of Perfection. How much longer will Hope dance on my intellect?

Miss Igoe told me of a picture she had taken on a rock at Panama, N. Y. There were several others in the group, interpolated so as to dilute the effect of Mina's beauty, as she stated the picture was taken *on a rock*. I immediately brought my scientific imagination to work to ascertain how the artist could have flowed collodion over a rock and put so many people inside his camera. Miss Igoe kindly corrected her explanation by stating that a picture was taken by a camera of a group on a rock. Thus my mind was brought back from a suspicion of her verbal integrity to a belief in the honesty of her narrative.

After supper Mrs. G, Daisy and Louise, with myself as an incidental appendage, walked over to the town of Ocean Spray, went into a drug store and bought some alleged candy, asked the gilded youth with the usual vacuous expression if he had any nitric peroxide. He gave a wild stare of incomprehensibility. Then I simplified the name to nitric acid, which I hoped was within the scope of his understanding. A faint gleam of intelligence crept over his face, whereupon he went into another room, from which he returned with the remark that he didn't keep nitric acid. Fancy a drug store without nitric acid. A drug store nowadays seems to consist of a frontage of red, blue and green demijohns, a soda fountain, case with candy and toothbrushes, a lot of almost empty bottles with death and stomachatic destruction written in Latin on them, all in charge of a young man with a hatchet-shaped head, hair laid out by a civil engineer, and a blank stare of mediocrity on his face that by comparison would cause a gum Indian in the Eden Musée to look intellectual.

On our return I carried the terrealbian gum drops. Moon was shining brightly. Girls called my attention several times to beauty of the light from said moon shining upon the waters. Couldn't appreciate it, was so busy taking a mental triangleation of the moon, the two sides of said triangle meeting the base line of the earth at Woodside and Akron, Ohio.

Miss Igoe told us about her love of ancient literature, how she loved to read Latin but couldn't. I told her I was so fond of Greek that I always rushed for the comedies of Aristophanes to read whenever I had the jumping toothache.

Woodside Villa
July 20, 1885

Arose before anybody else. Came down and went out to look at Mamma Earth and her green clothes. Breakfasted. Read aloud from Madame Recamier's memoirs for the ladies. Kept this up for an hour. Got as hoarse as a fog horn. Think the ladies got jealous of Madame Recamier.

It's so hot I put everything off. Hot weather is the mother of procrastination. My energy is at ebb tide. I'm getting caloricly stupid. Tried to read some of the involved sentences in Miss Cleveland's book. Mind stumbled on a ponderous perioration and fell in between two paragraphs and lay unconscious for ten minutes. Smoked a cigar under the alias of Rena Victoria. Think it must have been seasoned in a sewer. Mrs. Clark told me a story about Louise's mother singing in a company a song called I have no home, I have no home. Somebody halloed out that he would provide her with a good home if she would stop. I understood Mrs. Clark to say that this gentleman was a bookkeeper in a smallpox hospital. Mrs. G has placed fly paper all over the house. These cunning engines of insectiverous destruction are doing a big business. One of the first things I do when I reach heaven is to ascertain what flies are made for. This done, I'll be ready for business. Perhaps I am too sanguine and may bring up at the other terminal and one of my punishments will be a general ukase from Satan to keep mum when Edison tries to get any entomological information. Satan is the scarecrow in the religious cornfield.

Towards sundown went with the ladies on yacht. Talked about love, cupid, Apollo, Adonis, ideal persons. One of the ladies said she had never come across her ideal. I suggested she wait until the second Advent. Damon steered the galleon. Damon's heart is so big it inclines him to embonpoint. On shore it was hot enough to test safes. But on the water 'twas cool as a cucumber in an arctic cache. Mrs. G has promised for three consecutive days to have some clams à la Taft. She has perspired her memory all away.

Been hunting around for some ants' nests so I can have a good watch of them laying on the grass. Don't seem to be any around. Don't think an ant could make a decent living in a land where a Yankee has to emigrate from to survive. For the first time in my life I have bought a pair of premeditatedly tight shoes. These shoes are small and look nice. My No. 2 mind (acquired mind) has succeeded in convincing my No. 1 mind (primal mind or heart) that it is pure vanity, conceit and folly to suffer bodily pains that one's person may have graces the outcome of secret agony. Read the funny column in the Traveller and went to bed.

Woodside Villa
July 21, 1885

Slept splendid. Evidently I was inoculated with insomnic bactilli when a baby. Arose early, went out to flirt with the flowers. I wonder if there are not microscopic orchids growing on the motes of the air. Saw big field of squashes throwing out their leafy tentacles to the wind, preparing to catch the little fleeting atom for assimutation into the progeny of the squash gourd. A spider weaves its net to catch an organized whole. How like this is the living plant. The leaves and stalk catch the primal free atom. All are then arranged in an organized whole.

Heard a call from the house that sounded like the shriek of a lost angel. It was a female voice three sizes too small for the distance, and was a call for breakfast. After breakfast laid down on sofa, fell into light draught sleep, dreamed that in the depth of space on a bleak and gigantic planet the solitary soul of the great Napoleon was the sole inhabitant. I saw him as in the pictures—in contemplative aspect with his blue eagle eye, amid the howl of the tempest and the lashing of gigantic waves high up on a jutting promontory gazing out among the worlds and stars that stud the depths of infinity. Miles above him circled and swept the sky with ponderous wing the imperial condor, bearing in his talons a message.

Then the scene busted. This comes from reading about Napoleon in Madame Recamier's memoirs. Then my dream changed. Thought I was looking out upon the sea. Suddenly the air was filled with millions of little cherubs as one sees in Raphael's pictures. Each, I thought, was about the size of a fly. They were perfectly formed and seemed semi-transparent. Each swept down to the surface of the sea, reached out both their tiny hands and grabbed a very small drop of water, and flew upwards, where they assembled and appeared to form a cloud. This method of forming clouds was so different from the method described in Ganot's Physics that I congratulated myself on having learned the true method and was thinking how I would gloat over the chagrin of those cold-blooded Savants who would disect an angel or boil a live baby to study the perturbations of the human larynx. Then this scheme was wrecked by my awakening.

The weather being cool, went out on veranda to exercise my appreciation of nature. Saw bugs, butterflies as varied as Prang's chromos. Birds innumerable, flowers with as great a variety of color as calico for the African market. Then to spoil the whole two miserable mortals came who probably carry the idea that this world was created for them exclusively and that a large portion of the Creator's time was specially devoted to hearing requests, criticism and complaints about the imperfection of the natural laws which regulate this mud ball. What a wonderfully small idea mankind has of the almighty! My impression is that he has made unchangeable laws to govern this and billions of other worlds, and that he has forgotten even the existence of this little mote of ours ages ago. Why can't man follow up and practice the teachings of his own conscience, mind his business, and not obtrude his purposely created finite mind in affairs that will be attended to without any volunteer advice?

Came into the house at the request of the ladies and read aloud for two hours from the Memoirs Recamier. Then talked on the subject of the tender passion. The ladies never seem to tire of this subject. Then supper. Some *Trovotores du Pave* made their appearance and commenced to play. I requested the distinguished honor of their presence on the veranda. After supper, weather being cool but rather windy, took our trovotores on the yacht and all hands sailed out on the bay. Had to go around an arm of the bay to get coal. Water splashed so I got dashed wet. There several times the water broke loose from the iron grips of gravitation and jumped on my sixty-five-dollar coat. But when one of the ladies got a small fragment of a drop on her dress orders were issued to make for port. Landed and took our trovotores to house. Several ladies hiring houses for the summer brought their husbands with them and helped sop up the music. Afterwards Mrs. and Mr. G hospitabalized by firing off several champagne bottles and some of those delightful cookies. I do believe I have a big bump for cookies. The first entry made by the recording angel on my behalf was for stealing my mother's cookies.

Eleven o'clock came and the pattering of many footsteps upon the stairs signaled the coming birth of silence, only to be disturbed by the sonorous snore of the amiable Damon and the demonic laughter of the amatory family cat.

Sundry Observations

In the year 1887, the idea occurred to me that it was possible to devise an instrument which should do for the eye what the phonograph does for the ear, and that by a combination of the two, all motion and sound could be recorded and reproduced simultaneously. This idea, the germ of which came from the little toy called the Zoetrope, and the work of Muybridge, Marié, and others has now been accomplished, so that every change of facial expression can be recorded and reproduced life size. The Kinetoscope is only a small model illustrating the present stage of progress, but with each succeeding month new possibilities are brought into view. I believe that in coming years by my own work and that of Dickson, Muybridge, Marié and others who will doubtless enter the field, that grand opera can be given at the Metropolitan Opera House at New York without any material change from the original, and with artists and musicians long since dead. The following article which gives an able and reliable account of this invention has my entire endorsation. The authors are peculiarly well qualified for their task from a literary standpoint and the exceptional opportunities which Mr. Dickson has had in the fruition of the work.

                    Thomas A. Edison

4. FACSIMILE OF EDISON'S HANDWRITING

I
Autobiographical

AUTOBIOGRAPHICAL

I

IN TRYING to perfect a thing, I sometimes run straight up against a granite wall a hundred feet high. If, after trying and trying and trying again, I can't get over it, I turn to something else. Then, someday, it may be months or it may be years later, something is discovered either by myself or someone else, or something happens in some part of the world, which I recognize may help me to scale at least part of that wall.

I never allow myself to become discouraged under any circumstances. I recall that after we had conducted thousands of experiments on a certain project without solving the problem, one of my associates, after we had conducted the crowning experiment and it had proved a failure, expressed discouragement and disgust over our having failed "to find out anything." I cheerily assured him that we *had* learned something. For we had learned for a certainty that the thing couldn't be done that way, and that we would have to try some other way. We sometimes learn a lot from our failures if we have put into the effort the best thought and work we are capable of.

I-1921

II

I BECAME DEAF when I was about twelve years old. I had just got a job as newsboy on the Grand Trunk Railway, and it is supposed that the injury which permanently deafened me was caused by my being lifted by the ears from where I stood upon the ground into the baggage car. Earache came first, then a little deafness, and this deafness increased until at the theater I could hear only a few words now and then. Plays and most other "entertainments" in consequence became a bore to me, although I could imagine enough to fill in the gaps my hearing left. I am inclined to think I did not miss much. After the earache finally stopped I settled down into steady deafness.

There were no great specialists, I presume, in that region at the time, but I had doctors. They could do nothing for me.

I have been deaf ever since and the fact that I am getting deafer constantly, they tell me, doesn't bother me. I have been deaf enough for many years to know the worst, and my deafness has been not a handicap but a help to me.

From the very start, after the pain ceased, deafness probably drove me to reading. To compare the affliction of deafness with that of blindness is absurd, in spite of the fact that blind people usually seem rather above the average of happiness.

My refuge was the Detroit Public Library. I started, it now seems to me, with the first book on the bottom shelf and went through the lot, one by one. I didn't read a few books. I read the library. Then I got a collection called "The Penny Library Encyclopedia" which was published in Dublin, and read that through.

I read Burton's "Anatomy of Melancholy"—pretty heavy reading for a youngster. It might have been, if I hadn't been taught by my deafness that almost any book will supply entertainment or instruction. By the time I tackled "The Anatomy of Melancholy" I could enjoy any good literature, and had found that there was virtually no enjoyment in trash. Following the Anatomy came Newton's "Principles."

Amidst a wilderness of mathematics there were intervals of ordinary English literature of the better kind. But I kept at mathematics till I got a distaste for it. In that time I had all I really needed, but I had not carried my development as far as I had meant to.

That reading was the only education I ever had in mathematics, and I am not a mathematician, but I can get within ten per cent in the higher reaches of the art. I remember an expert employed by Smith, Fleming & Company, a great Scotch firm of merchants, whom I, when I was rather young, had been sent across to see * in regard to some experiments con-

* This trip to England was in 1873.

nected with the ocean cable. I got to talking with that expert concerning a problem of static. He worked four hours. I worked only half an hour and was only ten per cent out, which was right enough for my purposes.

While I was a newsboy on the Grand Trunk I had a chance to learn that money can be made out of a little careful thought, and, being poor, I already knew that money is a valuable thing. Boys who don't know that are under a disadvantage greater than deafness. That was a long time ago. The Civil War was on and the Battle of Pittsburgh Landing, sometimes called the Battle of Shiloh, was in progress—and I was already very deaf. In my isolation (insulation would be a better term) I had time to think things out. I decided that if I could send ahead to outlying stations a hint of the big war news which I, there in Detroit, had learned was coming, I could do a better than normal business when I reached them.

The combat, we in Detroit knew, was terrific. The bulletins would apprise the people of it. They would be eager for the newspapers telling how sixty thousand men had fallen among the armies of the North and South.

I therefore ran to the office of the Detroit Free Press and asked Mr. Seitz, the man in charge, if he would trust me for a thousand newspapers. He regarded me as if perhaps I might be crazy, but referred me to Mr. Story. Mr. Story carefully considered me.

I was poorly dressed. He hesitated, but finally told Mr. Seitz to let me have the papers.

I got them to the station and into the baggage car as best I could and then attended to my scheme. All along the line I had made friends of the station-agents, who also were the telegraphers, by giving them candy and other things which a train-boy dealt in in those days. They were a good-natured lot of men, too, and had been kind to me. I wired ahead to them, through the courtesy of the Detroit agent, who also was my friend, asking them to post notices that when the train arrived I would have newspapers with details of the great battle.

When I got to the first station on the run I found that the device had worked beyond my expectations. The platform literally was crowded with men and women anxious to buy newspapers. After one look at that crowd I raised the price from five cents to ten and sold as many papers as the crowd could absorb. At Mount Clemons, the next station, I raised the price from ten cents to fifteen. The advertising worked as well at all the other stations. By the time the train reached Port Huron I had advanced the price of the Detroit Free Press for that day to thirty-five cents per copy and everybody took one.

Out of this one idea I made enough money to give me a chance to learn telegraphy. This was something I long had wished to do, for thus early I had found that my deafness did not prevent me from hearing the clicking of a telegraph instrument when I was as near to it as an operator always must be. From the start I found that deafness was an advantage to a telegrapher. While I could hear unerringly the loud ticking of the instrument, I could not hear other and perhaps distracting sounds. I could not even hear the instrument of the man next to me in a big office. I became rather well-known as a fast operator, especially at receiving.

It may be said that I was shut off from that particular kind of social intercourse which is small talk. I am glad of it. I couldn't hear, for instance, the conversations at the dinner tables of the boarding-houses and hotels where after I became a telegrapher I took my meals. Freedom from such talk gave me an opportunity to think out my problems. I have no doubt that my nerves are stronger and better today than they would have been if I had heard all the foolish conversation and other meaningless sounds that normal people hear. The things that I have needed to hear I have heard.

I think it is because my nerves have not been bothered that now I am able to write without tremor. Few men of my age can do that. Steady nerves are perhaps an advantage of themselves great enough to offset impaired hearing. To me, when I go over there from Orange, New York seems rather a quiet place. Not even that city is a strain upon my nerves. Most nerve strain of our modern life, I fancy, comes to us through our ears.

When the Ninth Avenue Elevated Railway first began its operation in New York there was much complaint about its noisiness. Some people were literally up in arms. I was hired to go to the metropolis to make a report on it. The fact that my hearing was not perfect enabled me to find out what the trouble really was. I heard only the worst of it, you understand, and this helped me to determine that the difficulty lay in the rail joints. Other experts had not been able to make sure of that because they had heard too much general uproar to make it possible for them to make sure of details.

People with good hearing have become so accustomed to the uproar of civilization that that uproar has become necessary to their lives. If all noise suddenly should stop on Broadway, Broadwayites would faint away. Broadway as it is is a peaceful thoroughfare to me.

A man talking in a boiler-shop multiplies the volume of his voice by four or five times and yet finds it difficult to make the man of normal hearing understand. But I can hear talk in such noisy places without much difficulty. When I traveled much between New York and Orange on suburban trains, while the train was running at full speed and roaring at its loudest, I would hear women telling secrets to one another, taking advantage of the noise. But during stops, while those near to me conversed in ordinary tones, I could not hear a single word.

I have an idea that for many years my ears have suited the conditions of modern city life better than the average man's. But in the country or the quiet suburbs, the situation is reversed. There the man with normal hearing has a great advantage over me. For instance, I haven't heard a bird sing since I was twelve years old. But I can hear anything upon the phonograph.

I know men who worry about being deaf although they are not half as deaf as I am. Study of these men will indicate that they enjoy the unimportant. They would like keen hearing when they sit at table where foolish gossip flies about. They regret that they are missing nonsense. If they would let their deafness drive them to good books they would find the world a very pleasant place.

Some years ago a specialist came to me and informed me that he could improve my hearing. I presume he might have done it. But I wouldn't let him try.

I continually experiment with the phonograph, constantly improving it. There are those who fear that radio will kill it as a salable device, but I know better. People will continue to want to hear what they want to hear when they want to hear it. They will continue to prefer what they hear without rather than with static and other interruptions and distractions. They will continue to desire to have carefully selected voices and well-chosen instrumentalists ready for their entertainment, rather than to trust to luck and the program-arranger at a broadcasting station.

My eyes have always been extremely good. All the extensive experimentation I have done with arcs and other brilliant lights seems not to have hurt them at all.

I read three newspapers each day. If they are delayed or do not reach me I don't know what to do. The vast development of the newspaper and magazine has done more even than the motion picture to make hearing unnecessary.

Long ago nature began to make the hearing of human beings less acute than it had been in their earlier development. Nature always knows her business. The man engaged in firing fourteen-inch guns carefully plugs up his ears before he pulls the lanyard. There are analogies in many lines where ears are not actually plugged. In some instances they are not plugged when they might better be. I have heard people who live in towns of, say, two or three thousand, say that the Sunday quiet is depressing. Such people have achieved the noise habit. It is like the drug habit.

We need light and sight in order to get information without which mental development would be very difficult, although possible, as witness Helen Keller, who has had neither sight nor hearing since her early childhood and yet is a highly educated woman. I went through Switzerland in a motor-car, so that I could visit little towns and villages, and noted the effect of artificial light on the inhabitants. Where water-power and electric light had been developed everyone seemed normally intelligent. Where these appliances did not exist and the natives went to bed with the chickens, staying there till daylight, they were far less intelligent.

Once I was elected to membership in a certain business organization. I went to its dinners where there was much speech-making. At first I regretted that I could not hear those often long orations. Then, one year, they printed them after the dinner and I read them. I haven't felt a mite of sorrow since.

A man went up to Sing Sing—a reformer. One of the listening convicts—not in the least deaf—got uneasy after half an hour and yelled, disturbing the whole meeting. A warden promptly knocked him senseless and the orator went on. The convict woke up after another thirty minutes and, finding that the speaker was still at it, begged the warden to knock him out again.

When the other day, I read that a certain scientist had developed a short-term anesthetic, the first thought that came to me was that it should be served out at banquets to people with good hearing.

We are building a world in which the person who is deaf will have a definite advantage. If we keep on as we are going we shall have a general environment which will be impossible to the acutely hearing person. Normal individuals have their troubles even now. Fast cars without mufflers and the whirr of airplanes must definitely affect nerves. They do not and they could not bother mine or those of any other deaf person.

Deafness has done many good things for the world. In my own case it has been responsible, I think, for the perfection of the phonograph; and it had something to do with the development of the telephone into usable form. When Bell first worked out his telephone idea I tried it and the sound which came in through the instrument was so weak I couldn't hear it. I started to develop it and kept on until the sounds were audible to me. I sold my improvement, the carbon transmitter, to the Western Union and they sold it to Bell. It made the telephone successful. If I had not been deaf it is possible and even probable that this improvement would not have been made. The telephone as we now know it might have been delayed if a deaf electrician had not undertaken the job of making it a practical thing.

The phonograph never would have been what it now is and for a long time has been if I had not been deaf. Being deaf, my knowledge of sounds had been developed till it was extensive and I knew that I was not and no one else was getting overtones. Others working in the same field did not realize this imperfection, because they were not deaf. Deafness, pure and simple, was responsible for the experimentation which perfected the machine. It took me twenty years to make a perfect record of piano music because it is full of overtones. I now can do it—just because I'm deaf.

My deafness has been a definite advantage in my business, too, in more ways than one. The fact that I do not rely on verbal agreements and reports is one reason for this. There would be a chance that I might not hear them perfectly. So I have everything set down in black and white. That has saved me certain difficulties which I might have had if I had been acute of hearing. My deafness never has prevented me from making money in a single instance. It has helped me many times. It has been an asset to me always.

Even in my courtship my deafness was a help. In the first place it excused me for getting quite a little nearer to her than I would have dared to if I hadn't had to be quite close in order to hear what she said. If something had not overcome my natural bashfulness I might have been too faint of heart to win. And after things were actually going nicely, I found hearing unnecessary.

My later courtship was carried on by telegraph. I taught the lady of my heart the Morse code, and when she could both send and receive we got along much better than we could have with spoken words by tapping our remarks to one another on our hands. Presently I asked her thus, in Morse code, if she would marry me. The word "Yes" is an easy one to send by telegraphic signals, and she sent it. If she had been obliged to speak it she might have found it harder. Nobody knew anything about many of our conversations on a long drive in the White Mountains. If we had spoken words, others would have heard them. We could use pet names without the least embarrassment, although there were three other people in the carriage. We still use the telegraphic code at times. When we go to hear a spoken play she keeps her hand upon my knee and telegraphs the words the actors use so that I know something about the drama though I hear nothing of the dialog.

Every branch of education can be taught through books and motion pictures. Films already have done much to mold the public, young and old. They have affected commerce, too. We all wear English motor caps because we liked them when we saw them in the motion pictures. Australians buy American shoes because they have seen and liked them in motion pictures. Presently European clothing will predominate among the Asiatics in India, Japan and China because the natives of these lands have seen it in the motion pictures. I believe immensely in the phonograph, but talking-machines can never do what motion pictures can do in forming the thought and habits of the whole world.

And finally: The best thinking has been done in solitude. The worst has been done in turmoil.

IV-1925

III

I'M FREE to confess that I read two morning papers and three evening papers, all the principal magazines, except the fiction part, and most of the scientific publications. Sometimes when loafing I take a dip into a detective story. You know, Macaulay did that, too.

I do think that a young man should always read a daily newspaper. If he is going into business in New York he should read in addition the New York Journal of Commerce. If he is an electrical engineer he should read a journal on engineering, and so on throughout the field. We live and grow by new knowledge.

I generally recommend only those books that are written by men who actually try to describe things plainly, simply and by analogy with things everybody knows. I am sorry to say that ordinary scientific books are in nearly every case written by men who have no capacity to explain anything. But, after all, the masterpieces in any field are mighty few.

Progress is the thing that puts most books in the discard. Nearly all my books are transactions of scientific societies, which will never be republished. They gain in value constantly on account of the scarcity of the earlier volumes. I have made a rough estimate, based on actual purchases, that they gain, say, about two per cent per annum in value. It is sometimes said that the societies publish too much, but I don't think so—provided it is real information.

I use these books to prevent waste of time, and money, by not doing again the things that have already been done or tried out by others—unless you want to make the experiment again, just as you like to hear a piece of music again. See how Faraday's works are crammed with the simple report of test and discoveries, his record being like that in the very rocks. Look at the recent reprint in five or six languages, including the original Latin, of Oersted's great determinations in electro-magnetism. It's awfully short, but there is literally an experiment and a fact in every line. Such is truth forever.

II-13-1921

IV

I HAVE BEEN asked what a man over seventy can do to keep occupied. The trouble is, that a man who can't keep busy didn't take interest in a great number of things when he was mentally active in his younger years. If he had done so, he would find plenty to occupy his time in reading, observing and watching people. There are a great many hobbies he can work with and keep busy until his death.

I'm seventy-four, and I don't want to retire. When

the doctor brings in the oxygen cylinder, I'll know it's time for me to give up.

Men are not as active at seventy as they were at fifty because they hurt their machinery too much. If they like a certain thing, they will overdo it. They eat too much, or drink too much, or if they like sleeping they will sleep too much.

11-11-1921

V

As HUMAN beings are now constituted, it is impossible for them to be very happy. The only ones who are continuously happy are the ones who, having little ambition, do small things of little importance. A man whose business it is to catch butterflies is probably pretty happy all of the time.

The happiest time in my life was when I was twelve years old. I was just old enough to have a good time in the world, but not old enough to understand any of its troubles, Looking back now, across eighty-two years, I can see that relatively I have been happy. I have had a better chance to be happy than have most people. But I have had plenty of unhappiness, too.

But I have always found, when I was worrying, that the best thing to do was to put my mind upon something, work hard and forget what was troubling me. As a cure for worrying, work is better than whisky. Much better.

Human beings, as they are now constituted, are unable to be very happy, because, no matter how much they have, they want more. I refer now to material things—to money and the luxuries of life.

For a good many years I worried about my payroll; didn't always know how I was going to meet it. My trouble has been that I have always had too much ambition and tried to do things that were sometimes financially too big for me. If I had not had so much ambition and had not tried to do so many things I probably would have been happier, but less useful.

1930

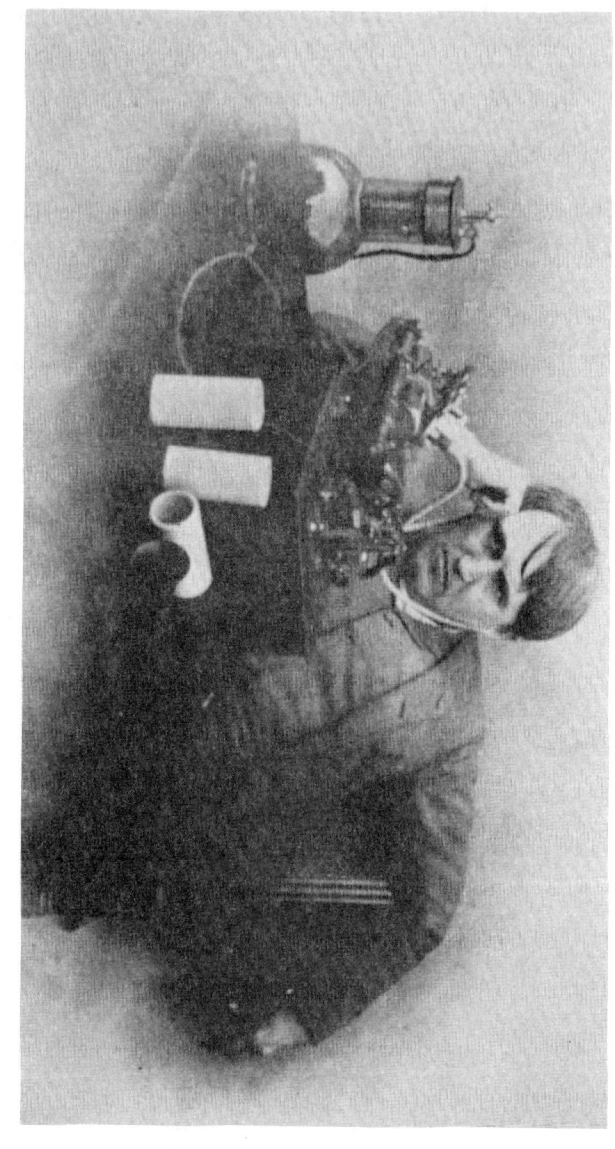

3. EDISON WITH HIS FIRST WAX PHONOGRAPH

II
Moving Pictures and the Arts

I. "BLACK MARIA" EDISON'S FIRST MOTION PICTURE STUDIO

MOVING PICTURES AND THE ARTS

VI · MONEY AND MOVIES

THEY SAY they are spending a million dollars nowadays to make just one big picture. If I had been told in the days of our first movie studio that anybody would spend a million dollars to produce a single film, I don't know whether I would have swallowed it or not. It would have been some effort.

It may seem curious, but the money end of the movies never hit me the hardest. The feature that did appeal to me about the whole thing was the educational possibilities I thought I could see. I had some glowing dreams about what the camera could be made to do and ought to do in teaching the world things it needed to know—teaching it in a more vivid, direct way.

I figured that after the novelty wore off the camera would either be taken up by the big educators and pushed as a new agency in the schools—or that it would be developed mostly along straight amusement lines for entertainment and commercial purposes. I guess up to date the entertainment and commercial purposes have won.

I don't know about the quality of the entertainment always, but I suspect there has been good money in it—for those who knew their business. When the industry began to specialize as a big amusement proposition I quit the game as an active producer.

A good many people seemed to wonder why I did so—maybe they still wonder. But the answer is simple enough. I was an inventor—an experimenter. I wasn't a theatrical producer. And I had no ambitions to become one.

If, on the other hand, the educational uses of the camera had come more to the front, as I had hoped, and I had seen an opportunity to develop some new ideas along those lines, my story as a producer might have been very different. I should have been far more interested in going on.

Do you know that one of my first thoughts for the motion picture camera was to combine it with the phonograph? In fact, that was what primarily interested me in motion pictures—the hope of developing something that would do for the eye what the phonograph did for the ear.

My plan was to synchronize the camera and the phonograph so as to record sounds when the pictures were made, and reproduce the two in harmony. As a matter of fact, we did a lot of work along this line, and my talking pictures were shown in many theatres in the United States and foreign countries. I even worked on the possibility of an entire performance of grand opera, for example, being given in this way.

Another thought I had was that such a dual arrangement might record both the lives and the voices of the great men and women of the world. Can you realize the tremendous impetus this would be to the study of history and economics?

They are producing pictures of this kind now, I understand, by photographing and reproducing the sound waves. We were working, of course, from an entirely different angle—but we had the first of the so-called "Talking Pictures" in our laboratory thirty years ago.

We might have developed them into a greater commercial circulation if we had kept on—but I was interested in the educational and not the entertainment field. When the educators failed to respond I lost interest. What I had in mind was a bit ahead of the times, maybe. The world wasn't ready for the kind of education I had pictured.

Maybe I'm wrong, but I should say that in ten years textbooks as the principal medium of teaching will be as obsolete as the horse and carriage are now. I believe that in the next ten years visual education—the imparting of exact information through the motion picture camera—will be a matter of course in all of our schools. The printed lesson will be largely supplemental—not paramount.

Let's see how visual education might work out in a practicable way. Suppose we take the development of the memory through the medium of the eye. Most of us have never learned how to use our eyes properly —and still fewer of us have ever learned how to remember properly the impressions that our eyes do register. Perhaps I can illustrate what I mean.

In the early days of the motion picture camera an especial problem for us was to find what kind of pictures people were most interested in. We were pioneers in a brand-new field. You must remember that at that time only a small percentage of the public had ever seen a motion picture film of any sort. And we soon discovered that our problem wasn't so much that of the showman as that of the experimenter, the educator.

An important fact that we ran up against right at the outset was the need to make our arrangement of scenes just as obvious and simple as possible. We found that if we didn't keep to an easy straight continuity it was difficult for many of the spectators to follow the picture at all. They hadn't been trained to visualize more than one thought at a time—and it seemed hard for some of them to do that. The average memory faculty had not been developed beyond the most elemental lines.

If one of the pretentious motion pictures of to-day, with its elaborate titles and multitude of characters and scenes, had been exhibited at that time it would probably have been a conspicuous failure. Half of the audience would have been hopelessly confused before it was finished.

If the motion picture has done nothing else it has been the greatest quickener of brain action that we have ever had. It has stirred up sluggish brain-cells as all of the printing presses in the world could not do.

It is easy enough to understand why, and yet this angle has probably never occurred to most of us. The motion picture has a definite physical impression to present to the eye, but it is an impression so swift that in order to register and apply it properly brain-cells that had not been used to hurried exercise had to learn to function far beyond any limits to which they had been accustomed. The automobile got us used to physical speed. It was the motion picture that got us used to mental speed.

Take the matter of motion-picture captions or titles as an example. When they were first used they required at least fifty per cent more footage than they do to-day. In other words, it needed half again as much time for the audience to read and assimilate them.

We used to experiment with stop-watches on various types of mentalities, trying to strike a fair average of time to allow for a given impression to register. We picked children and old persons, clerks, mechanics, business men, professional men, housewives, and exhibited titles with varying numbers of words.

When we showed more than six or eight words at a time it was a revelation to see how many failed to get any connected thought at all. It was necessary either to slow up the projection speed, or to increase the amount of printed footage so as to allow each title to remain on the screen about twice the time necessary for a reader of normal brain action to master it.

I believe that this kind of experiment, with elaborations, is now a favorite test with professional psychologists. We found some astonishing results by taking a group of children, without any regard to selection, and giving them an elemental course in memory-training, which consisted simply in showing a series of titles at graduated rates of speed, and asking the children to repeat them in order when they were finished.

In the course of even a few days a twenty-five or thirty per cent improvement was found. In some cases it was startling.

I'll venture to say that without a very substantial improvement in the thinking apparatus of our movie patrons over what it was—say twenty-five or thirty years ago—the massive productions that we now take as a matter of course would be out of the question.

II-21-1925

VII · THE BEGINNING OF MOTION PICTURES

IT WAS IN 1890 that we decided that we were far enough advanced in our plans for the development of animated photography to warrant a special building for our work, but it was such an ungainly looking structure when it was done, and the boys had so much sport with it, that we called it "The Black Maria."

Our studio was almost as amazing as the pictures we made in it. We were looking for service, not art. The building itself was about twenty-five by thirty feet in dimensions, and we gave a grotesque effect to the roof by slanting it up in a hunch in the center and arranging shutters that could be opened or closed with a pulley to obtain the greatest benefit from the light.

Then, in order to make certain of as long a working day as possible, we swung the whole building on pivots, like an old-fashioned river bridge, so it could be turned to follow the course of the sun. We covered it with tar-paper outside, and painted it a dead black inside to bring our actors into the sharpest relief. It was a ghastly proposition for a stranger daring enough to brave its mysteries—especially when it began to turn like a ship in a gale. But we managed to make pictures there. And, after all, that was the real test.

"The Black Maria" always reminded me of an Irishman who used to work for me in my early days when we were trying out a certain variation of the railroad telegraph system; that is, sending a message from an ordinary wire to and from a moving train. We were working with our apparatus down on Staten Island at the time, and my Irish friend—his name was King—was in charge of the crew on the line.

He was a good electrician, too, but for some reason

he had difficulty in making the system operate as it should. Strange to say, it worked like a charm when the train was running in one direction, but as soon as it started on its return trip troubles began. Although King would swear and tear his hair he couldn't fathom the source of the disturbance.

Finally, in disgust, he wrote me that the only solution he could think of was for me to run an axle under Staten Island so the island could be turned instead of the train! This was a good deal the same kind of problem we had with our old "Black Maria." But we couldn't very well control the sun. So we had to compromise, and fix up a contrivance to turn the studio.

We didn't use artificial lights in those days. We had to depend altogether on nature. Therefore, it was a case of literally having to follow up the sun so as to extract all the benefit we could from every fugitive ray. Crude methods, the modern film producer may say, but they gave us results and fairly continuous results, too.

The phonograph first suggested the motion picture camera. I had been working for several years on my experiments for recording and reproducing sounds, and the thought occurred to me that it should be possible to devise an apparatus to do for the eye what the phonograph was designed to do for the ear.

That was the broad purpose, but how to accomplish that purpose was a problem which seemed more impossible the longer I studied it. It was in 1887 that I began my investigations, and photography, compared to what it is to-day, was in a decidedly crude state of development. Pictures were made by "wet" plates, operated by involved mechanism. The modern dry films were unheard of.

I had only one fact to guide me at all. This was the principle of optics, technically called "the persistence of vision," which proves that the sensation of light lingers in the brain for anywhere from one-tenth to one-twentieth part of a second after the light itself has disappeared from the sight of the eye.

Ptolemy, the ancient Greek mathematician, first demonstrated this truth by means of a wooden wheel, painted with spots of red paint. As the wheel was whirled swiftly around, the spots on its surface apparently melted together and gave the effect of one continuous red streak, although when the wheel had stopped it was seen the spots had not changed their positions at all.

This fact served as the basic principle for various mechanical toys, creating the illusion of pictures that moved before the eyes of the beholder. A very simple contrivance of this kind was a spinning cardboard, revolving on a string. On one side was the picture of a man, and on the other side the picture of a galloping horse. As the card was spun, the man apparently leaped into the saddle of the horse, whereas what actually happened was that the revolutions of the card brought the second picture into view before the eye had lost the mental image of the first. I presume the inventor of the novelty made a good sum. He deserved to.

This same idea was later elaborated into a contrivance called the "Zoetrope" that was very popular when I was a young man. Around the inside lower rim of a cylinder affair, opened at the top, a series of related pictures was pasted, generally of a humorous character. As the cylinder was rapidly rotated, the wondering eye, glued to the opening in the top, was regaled with a succession of scenes presumed to have all of the appearance of life. The fact that most of the pictures were wood-cuts and that the action didn't always match at the right moment created at times a weird effect, but for years the Zoetrope was one of the most popular fads of the day.

The photographic art itself was beginning to languish, but even with its imperfections it remained for the camera to add the needed touch of finish and reality to the revolving pictures. The circumstances of how this came about were rather curious. Indeed, I don't think that many persons to-day, even connected with the film industry, are familiar with the facts of how photography contrived to introduce the semblance of motion in its product.

An Englishman of the name of Muybridge, who was an enthusiast on two subjects—cameras and racehorses—was visiting at his California farm Senator

Leland Stanford, who was also something of a "crank" on the subject of blooded trotters. During the visit the merits of a certain horse, owned by the Senator, came under discussion, Stanford contending for one fact, and his guest arguing for another. To settle the dispute Muybridge conceived an ingenious plan.

Along one side of the private race-course on the farm he placed a row of twenty-four cameras. Attached to the shutter of each, he fastened a long thread, which in turn was carried across the track, and then, to make sure of obtaining sharp exposures, he erected a white screen opposite to serve as a reflector. When all was in readiness the race-horse was turned loose down the track.

As it dashed past the rows of cameras the various threads were snapped, and a series of photographs, establishing each successive point in the "action" of the horse, were automatically registered. When they were developed they revealed for the first time a complete photographic record of the minutest details of a horse in actual motion, and Muybridge had the satisfaction of using them to win his argument.

He would have laid the pictures away in his private collection, but some one suggested trying the effect on a Zoetrope apparatus. The result was so startling that it created something of a public sensation. But, except as a novelty, there was little practicable benefit gained. To have made an actual motion picture, lasting even for the space of a single minute, at the rate of twelve exposures per second, the minimum for steady illusion, would have required, under the plan of Muybridge, seven hundred and twenty different cameras.

There were many problems connected with the first motion picture camera, but before everything else came the question of making a unit machine—that is, one where all of the exposures needed could be made with the same apparatus and through the same lens. And this at once brought up the second difficulty. Obviously, it was quite impossible to construct any single camera capable of the proper speed and mechanism required for the purpose, and use glass plates for the exposures. I saw at once these would have to be discarded entirely, and any experiments would have to start from a brand new point of departure.

We tried various kinds of mechanisms and various kinds of materials and chemicals for our negatives. The experiments of a laboratory consist mostly in finding that something won't work. The worst of it is you never know beforehand, and sometimes it takes months, even years, before you discover you have been on the wrong line all the time. First we tried making a cylindrical shell, something like an ordinary phonograph cylinder, and sensitizing the surface in the hope of obtaining microscopic photographs which could be enlarged.

These impressions would have been no larger than the point of a pin, if successful, and, of course, our plan involved a tremendous magnifying process to produce results. But we couldn't find a substance for coating the cylinder that was sensitive enough for our need. The old dry albumen that had been used by photographers we found would not do at all. Then we tried a gelatine bromide of silver emulsion, and for a little while it looked like it might work.

The first minute impressions were all right, and seemed clear enough for our purpose, but as soon as we undertook enlargements we saw we were stumped at the start. The bromide of silver was so coarse that all of the details of the negative were blotted out even in an eighth-of-an-inch size. We had to begin again, and this time we tried a different kind of mechanism with the idea of making larger pictures.

And again we found that we were wrong. Celluloid by this time was on the market—and we conceived the idea of a drum, over which a sheet of prepared celluloid was drawn, with the edges squeezed into narrow slots in the rim, like the old tin-foil phonograph. We had to take our pictures spirally, and they were so limited in size as a result that only the center of each could be brought into focus.

It was along about this point that George Eastman came into our experiments. I heard that he was working on a new kind of dry film, and asked him to come down and talk it over. The result was that his representative went back home to see what he could do in making a narrow strip of sensitized film that would operate on a roll. Without George Eastman I don't know what the result would have been in the history of the motion picture. The months that followed were a series of discouragements for all of us. While he was busy with the problem of chemicals we were busy with the problem of mechanics.

It is almost impossible for the layman to appreciate the extreme niceties of adjustment we had to overcome. Try to realize that we were dealing always with minute fractions of seconds. For instance, allowing forty-six exposures per second, as we did at first, we had to face the fact that the film had to be stopped and started again after each exposure. Now, allowing a minimum of $1/100$ part of a second for every impression that was registered, you can see that practically half of our time was already gone, and in the remainder of the time we had to move the film forward the necessary distance for the next exposures.

And all this had to be done with the exactness of a watch movement. If there was the slightest variation in the movement of the film, or if it slipped at any time by so much as a hair's breadth, this fact was certain to show up in the enlargements. Finally we completed a mechanism that allowed the film to be moved in the uniform ratio of one-tenth part of the time needed for a satisfactory exposure, and permitted from twenty to forty such exposures per second.

It looked as though we were finished, and we tried

the first roll of film jubilantly. Success was in our hands. But we had counted too soon.

The strips had been made in a one-half inch width that we thought was ample, but it was not enough. We had to make a larger size, allowing a one-inch surface for the emulsion, with a one-half inch margin for the perforations needed for the locking device that we used for starting and stopping the film.

This meant, of course, adjusting our mechanical apparatus also to carry the new-sized roll; but we did it at last, and soon the first of the new cameras was ready to show what it could do.

I didn't apply for the patent until two years later. I was very much occupied with other matters, and while we all congratulated ourselves on what we had accomplished, and knew we had an interesting and novel apparatus, we generally regarded it more or less as a curiosity with no very large practicable possibilities. It probably seems strange to the world now, but such was the fact, even after we had exhibited our first pictures.

These were shown originally in an apparatus that we christened "The Kinetescope," consisting of a cabinet equipped with an electrical motor and battery, and carrying a fifty-foot band of film, passed through the field of a magnifying glass. They attracted quite a lot of attention at the World's Fair in Chicago in 1893, but we didn't think much of it until we found that two Englishmen, who had been interested in the exhibit, finding that I had carelessly neglected to patent the apparatus abroad, had started an independent manufacture on a considerable scale.

Of course, it was too late then to protect myself, and I concentrated my efforts in devising a mechanism that would project the pictures on a screen before an audience. This consisted largely in reversing the action of the apparatus for taking the original pictures.

The main trouble we found here was the question of "flicker" and eye strain. It was necessary primarily to find and establish a uniform speed both for photographing and projecting the pictures. If we kept the number of exposures down too low it made the action jerky and hard to follow on the screen. Nearly all of our first pictures allowed from thirty to forty exposures per second, although the number has since been reduced down to from fifteen to twenty.

I consider that the greatest mission of the motion picture is first to make people happy . . . to bring more joy and cheer and wholesome good will into this world of ours. And God knows we need it.

Second—to educate, elevate, and inspire. I believe that the motion picture is destined to revolutionize our educational system, and that in a few years it will supplant largely, if not entirely, the use of text-books in our schools. Books are clumsy methods of instruction at best, and often even the words of explanation in them have to be explained.

I should say that on the average we get only about

two per cent efficiency out of school books as they are written to-day. The education of the future, as I see it, will be conducted through the medium of the motion picture, a visualized education, where it should be possible to obtain a one-hundred-per-cent-efficiency.

The motion picture has tremendous possibilities for the training and development of the memory. There is no medium for memory-building as productive as the human eye.

That is another basic reason for the motion picture in the school. It will make a more alert and more capable generation of citizens and parents. You can't make a trained animal unless you start with a puppy. It is next to impossible to teach an old dog new tricks.

I do not believe that any other single agency of progress has the possibilities for a great and permanent good to humanity that I can see in the motion picture. And those possibilities are only beginning to be touched.

XI 1922

VIII · ON MUSIC

OPERA SINGERS cannot make a success of concert work, and vice-versa, for the same reason that a pugilist is not an exponent of calisthenics. One versed in the latter art will exercise his muscles in a very systematic and strengthening way, but these movements are not conducive to landing knock-out blows, as are those of the pugilist. It is in the manner of training, as well as being a matter of gift. And the same thing applies in some measure to music.

One may have a very fine voice and be able to thrill an audience in grand opera, but when used in a church or concert hall the greatness of the notes reverberates to such a degree that one loses the quality of the voice. Few opera singers are able to bring their voices down to the softness of tones required for the church, the concert or the drawing room. Their voices have been trained to be heard above the din of a full orchestra, to soar above the dramatic acting and reach the audience in the proper volume to please the ear. The concert singer, on the other hand, has been trained to a purity of tone which carries without reverberation, and if the concert singer should attempt to sing in opera, the voice while no doubt perfect for the work for which it was trained, would scarcely be heard at all when merged with the crash of the orchestral music and noise of the audience.

Concert work requires a voice of much less volume, but greater purity of tone, as each note is to be distinguished clearly, unaided by the orchestra or dramatic effects produced by the stage settings. The concert artist has to rely solely upon the ability to please an audience, unaided. The power to do this successfully rests on a good voice, well used, clear enunciation and a pleasing personality, without the straining for effect. The American singer does better work on the concert stage, owing to the fact that the average American citizen possesses a head as well as a voice. It means hard work to become a good singer, and they are as scarce as good carpenters, and for much the same reason, because it necessitates practise.

Many of the greatest singers, those gifted with the sweetest voices, are Americans. They never should go abroad to study, for the reason that there are many good teachers in this country, and the method is different, which causes the pupil to unlearn what they may have spent years in acquiring. Music in any event should be sung in one's own tongue; it is the only true way to create the atmosphere necessary to sing successfully the music of one's own homeland.

Who, save a Southerner, can sing effectively "The Swanee River"? And I doubt whether even a Southerner of this day can sing it with all the old-time melody and pathos brought out by the singers of a generation ago. Those who sang this greatly loved ballad during the Civil War were the ones who could get every atom of sweetness out of it.

There are two slogans which I wish every musical magazine would print in the most conspicuous place in their publications. These are, first, "To begin with the extreme youth of America and teach them not only the love of good music, but also to play on some musical instrument, as well as cultivating the voice"; second, "The necessity of good teachers in America."

To go back to beginning with the youth of America, I feel sure that any child, if started to study playing the violin in its tender years, can be taught to play well on this instrument, while if it is not taken up until after they have reached the age of fifteen they never can be taught to play well, unless they have special talent.

The Germans have the reputation of being a musical race. Yet when one comes to trace the ancestral origin of the great musicians who have been born in that country, the number is really comparatively few. For example, there is a general impression that Beethoven was German, when, as a matter of fact, he was a Hollander. One reason why Germany has gained such a musical reputation is that few children are brought up without acquiring the art of playing on at least one musical instrument. In fact, nearly every German family has its own home orchestra. Think what a beautiful, marvelous America this would be were every child taught music. With an orchestra in every family, think what a protection to the home it would be. What sweeter or more inspiring sight could there be than to see a family gathered together in the lovely companionship of good music? The cabaret and dance hall would have to go out of business.

And now as to the necessity of good teachers to train the youth of America. It should be as much against the law for one to teach music unless fully capable and qualified as for a dentist to practice unless he has his diploma and license. I believe every teacher should have a license as well as a diploma. In fact, I consider the first of the greater importance. If a dentist should ruin a set of teeth, the damage in a way could be repaired by the use of false ones; but a beautiful voice, once ruined, can never be restored. This is a loss not only to the person who may possess the voice, but an even greater loss to the country.

The phonograph is the acid test of a voice, for it catches and reproduces the voice just as it is; in fact, it is nothing more nor less than a re-creation of the voice. If a singer can reproduce on the phonograph advantageously, then you may be sure that the voice can run the gamut of criticism on the concert stage. For while the phonograph is primarily a parlor or concert hall instrument, yet I have tested it out in the Metropolitan Opera House to good effect.

Indeed, we use large theatres for our "Tone Tests," as we call them, where the singer stands beside the phonograph and sings with a record he or she has previously made. Suddenly the singer stops, but the song goes on, and the audience cannot tell the difference except by noting that the singer's lips are closed. The singer takes up the song again at times, with the same result. These demonstrations have been given in theatres from Maine to California before hundreds of thousands of music lovers.

Again, it is here that the phonograph can be of infinite advantage to those desiring to book singers for their concerts, as they naturally should know just what they are getting before engaging their singers. For instance, the clubs in other cities, when wishing to engage talent, could very readily hear and judge not only the singer's voice but the entire repertoire of songs, and thus be able to select the music best suited to their own community.

VII-1920

IX · OUR MUSICAL FUTURE

A GREAT FAULT WITH MUSICIANS is that most of them have not studied the science of the instrument they profess to play. They never take the pains to determine the mechanism of the things which produce their art, and hence they fail to get the most out of them. For instance, I have heard pianists playing on instruments of which one key would vary extraordinarily in timbre from the adjacent key and yet be unaware of it. I admit that in piano this ignorance of the instrument is not so apparent or dangerous as in other instruments, for the piano is not a true musical instrument but is in fact a musical compromise. The notes are measured out for the player, and he is able to produce consonances and octaves exactly, because the maker of his instrument has measured them out for him.

This, however, is not so in many other instruments. Take the violin; it is utterly impossible to play true consonances and octaves on the violin or any stringed instrument, though most musicians are unaware of this. The fact is very easily explained. In a stringed instrument a movement of one ten-thousandth of an inch along the string changes the tone, and in order for a player to give an absolutely exact tone he would have to intone it within a tenth of the thickness of tissue paper. When a violinist plays single notes he can generally correct a slight falsity of intonation by an almost instantaneous turn of his finger. His auditors do not catch this tuning for it occurs so rapidly. In the case of octaves he may correct and hold the right tone in one note but he is utterly incapable of doing this with two notes, as two simultaneous actions are impossible to the human brain; hence one note remains untrue. Octaves on stringed instruments are highly unpleasant aurally and yet composers continue to write them and virtuosi to play them because they do not appreciate their ugliness.

An illustration which strengthens my belief in this failure of artists to know the materials with which they work was that of an American artist well known, who recently made some records for us. After they were finished I paid for them but destroyed the records. When she demanded my reason for this I told her she had high harmonics on her G string. I had her play for me again, and again the falsity was apparent to me although she was unable to discern it. Then I took her instrument and put the string under a microscope, discovering that the string had worn square.

It was only after I showed this to her and explained it that I could convince her of her fault.

The reactions to tone should be far more certain than those of color, because so many people are color blind, whereas far more persons respond to tone. It is the rare persons who can not be stirred emotionally by music, and only in a few cases have I found an actual avoidance of it. In our laboratories we have begun to conduct experiments aiming to ascertain the effects of music on the human mind, but thus far have not come to definite conclusions; although similarity in the results of the experiments points towards interesting theories. For instance, of 180 works with which we experimented, we found that eighty per cent of the most popular works were those of which the rhythms were more plastic and long drawn out: music which seems to make a definite emotional appeal.

Nowadays the trouble with determining the actual reaction of persons to music is that convention plays so large a part in their choice. Most persons like what they are told or supposed to like. Thus if our workmen are told that a record is by Caruso they invariably like it, while an unknown singer will find them indifferent. Often we do not tell them the singer or we even tell them a different singer, and the result is far different.

I have heard between sixty to seventy thousand tunes, I presume, in these years, but I never permit the author or the singer to be told to me before I hear the record so I listen to it without previous judgment.

From this form of musical measurement I have come to believe that there are two very distinct types of composing. The first is just composing, and the second is taking music "out of the air itself," as one might say, pure inspiration. In Beethoven, for instance, this latter kind of music predominates. What a vast amount of pure inspiration is here! One may listen to a continuous half hour of his music and feel that every note was not just composed but actually inspired. In Verdi, Rossini, too, there is much of this. Wagner's "Valkyrie," however, is outside either of these classifications. It is elemental! And in Puccini I find a strange combination both of this elemental quality and of just composition. It is where the composer has left the inspired moment pure and undistorted that we get music of truly lasting appeal.

It is with the children that we must work if we would turn this into a musical nation. Take Germany. The nation is not a musical one, certainly not as musical as our own. Brahms, of all their great composers, is really the only one we may count as a German. Beethoven, a Dutchman; Wagner, Mendelssohn, Meyerbeer—all Jews. Yet Germany has developed a vast love of music among the people for the simple reason that almost every child is taught some instrument. In a family each youngster is given a different instrument to learn and in the home there is cultivated a love of art which proves more alluring than our moving pictures, and how much more inspiring! That is what we must do here. It is not the schools or the teachers that have in their power the making of a musical nation, but the mothers. Newspapers and individuals should preach the gospel of teaching music to our youth in their homes, a different instrument to each child; all our musical problems will solve themselves. Do this and a noble musical future is assured our coming generations.

I-22-1921

III
War and Peace

WAR AND PEACE

X · ON ATOMIC ENERGY

There will one day spring from the brain of science a machine or force so fearful in its potentialities, so absolutely terrifying, that even man, the fighter, who will dare torture and death in order to inflict torture and death, will be appalled, and so will abandon war for ever.

My solution for war is not Peace Congresses alone. It is 'preparation.' Preparation, not provocation, and this preparation or preparedness may one day involve the discovery of some terrific force, some engine of war the employment of which would mean anihilation for the opposing forces. The way to make war impossible is for the nations to go on experimenting, and to keep up to date with their inventions, so that war will be unthinkable, and therefore impossible. War is the desperate, vital problem of our time.

War will never be made impossible until men are convinced by definite demonstration that it is impossible.

The next great war will be fought out with poison-gas. Gas and the aeroplane will be the decisive factors.

I am much interested in atomic energy, but so far

as I can see, we have not yet reached the point where this exhaustless force can be harnessed and utilized. There is nothing to hang the imagination on. It may come some day. As a matter of fact, I am already experimenting along the lines of gathering information at my laboratory here.

Before we manage to harness atomic energy, we shall solve other problems. We shall possibly utilize the motion of the earth through space. Another source of enormous power, already harnessed, is that of the volcano, and as a matter of fact they are already getting some thousands of horsepower from the volcanoes in the Apennines—the backbone of Italy.

So far as atomic energy is concerned, there is nothing in sight just now. Although to-morrow some discovery might be made. Some quite dissimilar but collateral problem might open up this field by accident. Very often it happens that a discovery is made whilst working upon quite another problem.

The energy could be turned into electricity and projected not only across the Atlantic, but flung from any part of the world to any other part. Neither the Atlantic nor anything else could interpose an obstacle. The force residing in such a power is gigantic and illimitable.

VIII-1922

XI · CHANCES OF WAR

IT MAY BE that the cumulative effect of aerial navigation will be to decrease the chances of war. If that proves to be the case then the airplane thus will have rendered the very greatest possible service. Some people feel quite sure of this.

Perhaps my own mind inclines in that direction, for I am convinced that wars not only will not cease but will be frequent until the controlling groups in all the countries conclude that war is far too hazardous an enterprise to be undertaken in any circumstance whatever. Occasional fighting will be inevitable while men believe that they can take the risks of it with any half way reasonable chance of winning an advantage for themselves. If wars are ever done away with, their cessation will not be due to sentimental arguments, but to the fact that science and invention may make war so dangerous to everyone concerned that the sheer patriotism of educated people in all nations, plus their common sense, will be universally against the stupid war idea. He would be a bold and even reckless man who would declare this to be true at present.

T-1927

XII · HARNESSING OF NEW POWERS

QUITE APART from atomic energy, the motion of the earth alone as it turns on its axis and sweeps through space would give us all the light, power, and heat that we want, and a thousand times over.

Some day, we may harness that motion. Not only that, but one day we may harness the rise and fall of the tides and imprison the rays of the sun.

There are those who thing the labour problem would cease to exist, but struggle is inherent in humanity, not only upon questions of wages and hours, but upon questions of infinitely greater import and sweep. It is certainly inherent between the man who has and the man who hasn't—between the 'Haves' and the 'Have-nots.' The coming of limitless cheap power, as it will one day come, will not change that inherent vital principle so deep in humanity which is the mainspring of evolution. However limitless such power, however easy of application, no human being can live long without work. Individuals, here and there, may do so for a time, but eventually the restless, struggling human will find work of one kind or another to do. The pleasure of idleness is one of the great superstitions of the world. Such work may not always take the same form—but it will be work, whatever its form.

VIII-1922

XIII · THE WARS OF TOMORROW

FUTURE WARS are going to be waged almost exclusively with airplanes, submarines and gas. Battleships will not count for much. Guns are very spectacular instruments for killing. They make a great noise and explosive shells blow great holes in the earth—but guns do not carry destruction over a broad area.

A bursting shell kills only those who are within a few feet of it. A single charge of such a gas as chemists now know how to make is sufficiently deadly to kill every man, woman and child in an area equivalent to five or six blocks.

That is why I say it would not be difficult to send a flock of airplanes over a city and kill every inhabitant within five minutes without breaking a pane of glass. All that is necessary is to make a gas that is very poisonous and very heavy. Heavy gas settles on the earth so that no one in the vicinity can escape it.

XI-23-1921

XIV · ON DISARMAMENT CONFERENCES

We are more favorably situated than any other nation in the world and that puts us in a delicate position, comparable with that of the rich man in the midst of poor men.

Here is a good thing to remember: We've got to keep as sane about peace as we should keep about war.

It would be as utterly unreasonable to expect actual frankness as it would be to expect actual unselfishness at such a meeting. Secret dealing cannot be prevented. I am not certain that it ought to be. It would require a group of supermen as delegates—or of inefficient and unpatriotic citizens of the represented nations.

We must be cautious in our judgment of these things. Acceptance of the responsibilities of government representation may of necessity transform an honest man into the opposite. Don't forget that this old world is just as human now as when the apple episode occurred in Eden.

The competent representative of any government is likely to think, and may be justified in thinking, when the interests of the country sending him are threatened, that the end justifies the means.

The war did not reveal the inner secrets of the governments. All sorts of strictly private understandings now exist affecting practically every portion of the world, no matter how much this may be denied by diplomats.

Entirely wrong impressions may arise out of too free discussion of things, which have not been accomplished, but are being worked for. I know that that is true in business. I know it must be true at meetings of the sort which will occur in Washington.

America must not expect too much of this conference on the limitation of armaments. Its agreements will be dependent upon circumstances. The people must realize this or they will meet with disappointment. The delegates will be the servants of their governments. Their agreements will be like those of trade representatives who meet and solemnly agree to programmes and then rush to the telegraph offices to notify their selling agents to cut prices.

The whole world is hard up. Knowing that this condition will persist for the period of reconstruction it will be glad to dodge taxation for war-machinery purposes. This period will last for at least five years more. While the world remains hard up, common sense will be much stimulated, for the world, we must remember, is but an aggregate of human beings. The man grown rich will do things which when he was pressed for money he would have known to be foolish.

If we all can agree to being sensible for a short time, while we are short of funds, that brief experience may educate us so fully to the beauties of good sense that in later years we will cling to it. And now, it must be borne in mind, the nations will agree to almost anything because, as matters are, the future is too terribly uncertain to make prophecy a pleasant task.

We are all happier when we look ahead with confidence. The world wants confidence. We must be careful not to lose the possibility of it by scaring men through asking them to make agreements reaching far beyond their ken into the future.

We must realize that nations will not willingly commit themselves too extensively.

If governments would realize this principle and then go on experimenting with death-dealing devices, ceaselessly, inexorably, without counting cost (experimenting doesn't cost much; it's manufacture in large quantities which swells taxation) the world soon would be full of such death-dealing devices as would make war utterly impossible. Soon all the general staffs would be found useless, because no general staff would find it possible to meet scientific achievements in devising instruments of death.

Then, when war came, if reasonably prepared to ward away the first threatened attacks, we could proceed with the construction in great numbers of the best available and most perfectly developed device as it might be at that particular moment.

But I know one procedure that might tend to lessen likelihood of wars. No competent government in the world ever ought to cease experimentation with war-making machinery and substances. This, I think, at this time, is especially true with regard to aviation and asphyxiating and other war gases.

That may sound bloodthirsty. As a matter of fact it is the common sense of a true man of peace. Experimentally every terrible way of war-making should be developed without pause or hindrance.

Bring about that situation and humanity is going to say:

"I think I'd better quit on killing and try peaceable negotiation."

If every nation knew that it could not attack another, and, to use a slang phrase, 'get away with it,' there would be an end of arrogance. I feel sure that through experiments, utilizing present and approaching scientific knowledge to its full, such knowledge might be brought about.

At the end of a five-year period devoted to unceasing research and experiment another conference, at which knowledge of the dreadful potentialities revealed by such research would be well known or fully revealed, no matter how tremendously all experimenters tried to keep their results secret, would find the delegates more willing to be reasonable.

XI-6-1921

XV · THE FIGHT AGAINST RADICALISM

IT IS CURIOUS that the better impulses of our humanity do not work as hard to spread their careful, helpful thought as the less worthy elements do to spread their evil thought and foolish reasoning. If this could be reversed the world very quickly would become a better place to live in.

We hear a great deal in these days about radicalism, for example, and I have no doubt that the greater part of that which we hear is true. We are trying to fight this by locking up some dangerous people, deporting others and trying thus to warn them all.

With these methods I have not the slightest quarrel. Doubtless they are necessary. They may check the immediate dangers arising from constantly regrowing. It is conceivable that they may help.

Used alone certainly they won't permanently help us much. We must put soap-box orator against soap-box orator, if we wish, as the opponents of our present system do, to produce results, print pamphlet against pamphlet, in every conceivable way put argument against argument.

The best way to combat a campaign of miseducation is to conduct a campaign of education. The undesirables are gaining ground not because they are permitted to speak, print and scheme but because their falsities are uncontradicted. Putting a few of them in jail won't cure the evil, although I don't say keep them out of jail.

The thing which would destroy them utterly, making all their efforts unavailing with the American public, would be to prove them to that public to be liars. If we adopted tactics of that sort we could run them out of the country in a year. We wouldn't need to deport them; they would deport themselves, and be glad to have the chance to get away. A man will run a good deal faster from a hostile population than he will from a hostile Secret Service or police force.

We've got an immense foreign-born population to deal with. They don't read the English-language press, in which most of the arguments against radicalism are printed. Why should they be expected to? They don't know how, and it will be years before we can teach them to.

But most of them probably can read some language, and there are not so many languages that it would be impossible for the United States of America to use all of them as effectively as the radical workers and propagandists now use them.

These pests tell the ignorant man every day that he creates all wealth and is being robbed; presently he believes it. Nobody tells him that he isn't being robbed; and, while sometimes he is, usually he isn't. Those who try to tell the truth to him don't know how to reach his mind. They do not adapt themselves to him as the agitators do. Probably they don't make a living that way, while the blatherskites and Anarchists find it an easy way of getting money without working.

I can see no earthly reason why the sensible and constructive elements in American life should not publish the sensible and constructive facts of American life and hand them out out to my men as they leave the gates, as the Reds publish and hand out their arguments now.

I believe that the clean and right-thinking elements should work as hard as their opponents do, hiring able writers who would prepare articles disproving all the silly but curiously ably prepared twaddle of the agitators.

These men lie, lie daily, lie continually—and lie well.

But it never is a difficult thing to nail a lie if you know it is a lie, are informed about the truth and are willing to take the the trouble to tell your truth ably.

The workers of America, like the workers of the Allied countries (and perhaps more than some of them), are sound. Who can doubt it? They are showing far more common sense than their employers. We employers are a dead lot.

We ought to district the whole Nation, by groups of States, by States, by parts of States and by sections of the parts of States, and conduct a great campaign of education.

Before such a campaign had ended everybody, on both sides, would have learned something, and the more all of us know the better we shall be off as a Nation. Having done this, we should organize as carefully and minutely as we did for the loan drives and put that which we may find to say before the public in language plain and convincing.

It seems silly to me that the necessarily loosely organized, furtive and obviously not highly intelligent radicals should be permitted to conduct more competent campaigns of education than those conducted by potentially well organized, unafraid and highly intelligent constructionists.

If the people who now are yielding to the arguments of half truth or none had an opportunity to study with equal ease the real truth they would understand its genuineness and superiority. The trouble is that they have no such opportunity, and that chances for the study of false theories very cleverly presented, are at hand continually.

The cause of common sense sadly lacks leadership in this particular matter. It needs some young men like Roosevelt, perhaps, with both ability and energy, to start a real fight in the country and get other young men to stand beside him in keeping it up.

The Chambers of Commerce and other organizations which have practical reasons for desiring peace and progress along rational lines in the United States should come to life, get orators and get soap-boxes, and not only trail the Reds but precede them. Such procedure would wipe out all the nonsense, or as much of it as really is dangerous, in no time.

The worker needs some explanations from constructive minds. He's getting all he gets out of destructive minds. Let him understand that all these radicals are trying to make a fool of him (and measureably succeeding), and very soon he will turn on them. He's the only man who can discourage them. Let him understand what they really are after and he will not alone discourage, but destroy them.

At heart and head there are no better in the world than the workers of America. Let them once understand that they are being flim-flammed and loafing in the shops would stop. The strikes that are sending up the prices of necessities also would stop if our American workers comprehended the great fact that an idle man, whether he be a worker, or a millionaire, harms all.

II-1-1920

IV
Education and Work

EDUCATION AND WORK

XVI · EDUCATION AND SPEED

THE MOST NECESSARY TASK of civilization is to teach men how to think. It should be the primary purpose of our public schools. The world is moving too fast for them, they are cluttered up with too much red tape and precedent. We have too much red tape in all of our institutions.

Our educational system—much of it—belongs in the time when we traveled by horse-back and canal boat.

This is the age of speed—speed such as men had never dreamed before. We are annihilating distance—we are conquering not only the land and the sea but the air—we are doing in minutes what our grandfathers could not have done in days.

They were not equipped mentally to grasp or to utilize the new order of things which burst upon them. Many of them did not seem to know at first what it was all about. If modern industry and invention expected to have a market for its products it had to turn school-master on an elaborate scale. It had to educate the world before it could sell the world. It had to show men how to think a little farther and a little faster before it could expect to interest them in how to buy.

It was necessary to create an understanding and appreciation of a higher standard of living—and then a desire for it—a demand to get more out of life on the part of several million individuals who would have been entirely satisfied with what they had. People used to be content with tin bath tubs and kerosene lamps. Most of the attendants at the Chicago World's Fair of 1892 had never used a telephone. Had you told farmers who voted for Bryan for president that in less than twenty years they would be driving to town in automobiles at forty or fifty miles an hour they would have thought you had been drinking too much hard cider.

But the main point is that society was satisfied with things as they were. There could be no progress until enough people could be made dissatisfied—and this could be done only when they were brought to think beyond the limits to which they were accustomed. The educator had to follow the inventor—the specialist in high pressure stimulation of the public imagination—and the salesman had to wait until his work was done.

We may term it commercialized education—but it has made its results felt. I should say that the thinking power of the average man has increased perhaps twenty-five per cent in the past ten to twenty years. And certainly it has always been low enough.

It is astonishing what an effort it seems to be for many people to put their brains definitely and systematically to work. They seem to insist on somebody else —often anybody else—doing their thinking for them. That is why I regard the general mental stimulus we have seen in recent years as so significant. Several industrial factors have been definitely responsible—to mention only three of them, the motion pictures, the radio, and the automobile. Let us look at the automobile.

Most of us view the automobile principally as a great business and manufacturing achievement. It is —but it is a greater educational achievement.

Next to the World War it has done more, perhaps, to jar people out of the ruts of commonplace thinking than almost any other factor in our history. This is not so much because of its stimulus to our transportation as because of its stimulus to our **imagination.**

The great value of the automobile is not the fact that it has made it easier and quicker and cheaper to go to places but the fact that it has inspired several million people to go. It has caused them to move, to stir themselves, to get out and away, to wake up to what was going on about them. And any agency that would have moved some of them would be a public benefaction. Before the automobile it would have needed an earthquake. Many of them had never looked at a map since they left school.

We emphasize the slogan, "See America." But the

automobile has done more than that. It has made a good many hundred thousand Americans see themselves and their neighbors—for the first time. It has set their gray matter to work. It has revealed to them how petty and meaningless their lives were becoming.

In the beginning we were a pioneer people—a restless people. But when things came easier for us and we were able to make a comfortable living without much effort we began to lose our restlessness. The automobile is helping to restore it. And that is one of the most healthful signs of our generation. Restlessness is discontent—and discontent is the first necessity of progress. Show me a thoroughly satisfied man —and I will show you a failure.

The important mission of the automobile is not the opening up of new geography—but the opening up of new opportunity. And if it has awakened enough people to the fact, all of the gasoline we have used has not been too much.

The automobile has made better roads—but the best roads of progress it has made are not physical. They are those mystic paths which urge men into new worlds of imagination and incentive.

We have long since passed the age of the pedestrian. But the mental advance of society as a whole has not kept pace with our physical advance. We have come to take the wonders of invention as a matter of course—as we do everything else. But those who call this a sophisticated age are wrong. It is a perfunctory age. And it is so principally because the majority of people won't or can't think far enough to understand what it all means.

Physically, the world is moving faster than at any time since its creation and some of us may pause now and then to question our emphasis on physical speed, but if it serves to stir up our sluggish brain cells, if it makes it necessary for more of us to think in order to live, it is worth while.

The wheels of progress—especially those of the automobile—have worked results which might be called miracles. But their greatest service has been to raise the thinking capacity of society. If there is one evil in the world today for which there is no excuse it is the evil of stupidity.

Vol. 3, No. 6

XVII · OBSOLETE EDUCATION

I AM FREQUENTLY ASKED about our system of education. I say that we have none. Our system is a relic of past ages. It consists of parrot-like repetitions. It is a dull study of twenty-six hieroglyphs.

Groups of hieroglyphs. That is what the young of this present day study. Here is an object. I place it in the hands of a child. I tell him to look at it. If we begin before we have hardened and dried his mind he studies the object with kindling enthusiasm. The mind of the child is naturally active. Why should we make him take his impressions of things through the ear when he may be able to see? The child is a natural born "rubber neck." His curiosity is alert. Give him the chance and he will learn. One glance, if he sees the thing itself, is better than two hours of studying about a thing which he does not see. The child develops through exercise. Give him plenty of exercise for body and brain. The more he works his arm the bigger the muscles; the more the faculties are exercised in a normal way the greater the brain. The folds of the brain grow deeper through observation; they grow fallow from disuse. If we educate too abruptly—if we cram the mind with facts memorized for themselves alone—what comes? Pure atrophy. This matter of education is a big question for the American people. It is of the utmost importance that every faculty should meet its environment. What is the use of crowding the mind with facts which cannot be utilized by the child because the method of their acquisition is distasteful to him?

I like the Montessori method. It teaches through play. It makes learning a pleasure. It follows the natural instincts of the human being. That system of education will succeed which shows to those who learn the actual thing—not the ghost of it. I firmly believe that the moving picture is destined to bear an important part in the education of the future. One may devote pages to the descriptions of the processes of nature to be learned by rote in the schools. Suppose instead that we show to the child the stages of that process of nature—the cocoon itself, the picture of the cocoon unfolding, the butterfly actually emerging. The knowledge which comes from the actual seeing is worth while. The geography which comes from travel is better than the geography of the books; the next thing to travel is following the same scenes through the moving picture.

I am now conducting an educational experiment the results of which I shall announce one of these days. We have two classes, each consisting of twelve pupils under fifteen years of age. One is composed of girls and another of boys. They are being taught from moving pictures, and after seeing the pictures they write the results of their observations. We give them no formulae, no statements; we leave all to their own observation. The faculties are being quickened and stimulated by this method of study, which has in it an element of play as well, while the knowledge obtained is not from mere memorizing. There is much ignorance in the world, mostly from lack of proper observation. If we had a better system of education we should have hardly any room for "crooks."

The trouble with our way of educating as generally followed is that it does not give elasticity to the mind. It casts the brain into a mould. It insists that the child must accept. It does not encourage original thought or reasoning, and it lays more stress on memory than on observation. The result of accepting unrelated facts fosters conservatism. It breeds fear, and from fear comes ignorance. The seeing of things in the making is what counts. Then the mind can approach the gaining of knowledge without prejudice. Shall we say to the young that they shall merely memorize the observations of others, learn by rote the thoughts of others and, having spent years in the hoarding up of what we call knowledge, begin to think? The exercise in thinking should begin from the earliest years, and it can be directed through bringing the mind in contact with the things that are. What we call conservatism is largely a result of a hard and fast way of teaching, a worship of the twenty-six hieroglyphs, the adoration of symbols, which fosters the creed that nothing can be done which has not been done by our fathers. That is conservatism, which is the greatest foe of progress, for it is well known that it takes from five to seven years for every invention destined for universal use to make its way through the crust of tradition.

1-4-1914

XVIII · MEMORY TESTING

IT COSTS TOO MUCH to find out if a man is a good executive by trying him out on the job. So I made up my mind that we should have to have a formal test of some sort. This brought up the question of what we should look for; what is the most important qualification for an executive?

When I call upon one of my men for a decision, I

want it right away. When his department calls upon him for a decision, it wants it right away. It's all very well to say that you have got to look up the data on which the decision will be based, that you know just where to look, that data and decision will be forthcoming tomorrow afternoon. But I want the decision now; the department wants it now. It isn't convenient for me to wait, and certainly it isn't convenient for a whole department to hang in the air for an indeterminate period waiting for an executive to find something out that he might have had right in his head. My business is just like any other; when a decision is called for it must be forthcoming. And the man who is to make it must have all the pertinent facts.

On this ground it seemed to me that the very first thing an executive must have is a fine memory. I asked myself if I had ever heard of a high-class executive who lacked this qualification. I hadn't; have you? Of course you haven't. So I determined that I should test all candidates for executive positions by learning what I could about their memories.

Of course it does not follow that a man with a fine memory is necessarily a fine executive. He might have a wonderful memory and be an awful chump in the bargain. But if he has the memory he has the first qualification, and if he has not the memory he lacks the first qualification and nothing else matters. Even if after passing the memory test he turns out to be a failure and has to go, much motion and expense will have been saved by the immediate elimination of all candidates who lack this first requisite of memory.

The questionnaire that has attracted so much attention and been the target of much criticism was got up on this basis. The only way I know how to test a man's memory is to find out how much he has remembered and how much he has forgotten. Of course I don't care directly whether a man knows the capital of Nevada, or the source of mahogany, or the location of Timbuctoo. Of course I don't care whether he knows who Desmoulins and Pascal and Kit Carson were. But if he ever knew any of these things and doesn't know them now, I do very much care about that in connection with giving him a job. For the assumption is that if he has forgotten these things he will forget something else that has direct bearing on his job.

This memory of ours works in two ways. The things that are always before you, that you are continually conscious of knowing, comprise an insignificant part of the contents of your mental warehouse. Every moment of your life from the time you were old enough to perceive things at all, facts and facts and more facts have been sifting into your mind through the things you see and the things you hear and above all through the things you read—through your every contact with the external world. Millions and millions of facts which have come into your mind in this way ought still to be there. They stay down under the surface until you call for them—then if you have a good memory you find them popping right out. A man with a really fine memory of this type will often surprise himself by remembering a lot of things which he would not have supposed he had ever known, and which he can't for the life of him imagine how or when or where he learned.

If I tell you something now, and you know that I am going to ask you about it tomorrow and that it is going to be important for you to know, you are a poor creature indeed if you can't make yourself remember it. If I tell you something that interests you exceedingly, it is mighty strange if that doesn't stick, too. But that is not the kind of memory that counts. Don't come here for a job and tell me that you can remember anything you want to, anything you consider worth remembering. Out of every thousand facts that present themselves to you, I should think that at least 990 come unobtrusively, without the slightest indication whether they are to be of any subsequent importance to you or not. If your memory is a success, it will reproduce—within the proper limits of human fallibility, of course—any one of these items, when and where you want it.

Of course if I ask you 150 questions at random, I am going to strike some low spots in your knowledge. I am going to ask you some things that you never have known at all. No two people have precisely the same background of facts. But I do not expect anybody to answer every one of my questions. They are selected with the thought that they shall deal with things taught in schools and colleges—things that we have all had opportunity to learn, facts to which we have all been exposed during the course of our education and by our ordinary reading. Their subject matter is of no importance—they must merely be things that my applicants may fairly be assumed to have been taught at some time. Everybody must necessarily have been exposed to a very large majority of them. But if any candidate should answer every question on his paper, I should want to know where he got his advance copy of the questions! I am not looking for 100 per cent grades; but I am looking for, and I think I am entitled to expect, 90 per cent grades. A man who has not got 90 per cent of these facts at his command is deficient either in memory, as discussed already, or in the power of acquiring facts, as I shall presently make clear. And either deficiency is fatal for my purposes.

XI-1921

XIX · THE HABIT OF FORGETTING

Somewhere between the ages of eleven and fifteen, the average child begins to suffer from this atrophy, the paralysis of curiosity and the suspension of the power to observe. The trouble I should judge to lie with the schools, but its precise seat I would not venture to suggest. Perhaps it lies in a flagging interest, which leads quickly to the habit of listening without hearing, of looking without seeing—a habit which once fixed persists without regard to the existence or non-existence of interest. Whatever it is, it is clear to me that our schools and colleges are turning out men who not merely have failed to learn, but have been robbed of the capacity to learn.

If our schools would stiffen their standards, and find a means of holding the intellectually lazy average student of the present day to these stiffened standards, we should find, I think, that the system of learning today and forgetting permanently tomorrow would go out of fashion. If the set, formal examination were given less prominence I should think that would help too. A student must be of low caliber indeed if, with printed text and written notes before him covering the entire work of the term, he cannot cram enough facts into his head and keep them there long enough to get past the examination. When he has done this, so far as his present state of mind is concerned, he seems to be through with those facts—finished; he is never going to want them again, or worry about them. The habit of forgetting, the habit of not even taking things into his consciousness except under certain extraordinary conditions, is a vicious and a subtle one which he is not able to shake off.

XI-1921

XX · THE NEW GENERATION

THE OUTLOOK of to-day's youth is very different from that of the young people of the preceding generation. Their outlook differed from that which went before and this was equally true of each preceding generation. But the change which has occurred in the outlook of the rising generation is all in its favor. The youth of to-day does not deserve any especial credit for it. It is merely fortunate in the fact that, as is the case with all of us to-day, it is living in a different state of knowledge from that known to other generations. The very fact that it is youth guarantees it a greater benefit from this than age or even maturity can get. If the outlook of this generation were not different from that of the generation which preceded it this generation would be hopeless. The fact would demonstrate it to be dumb, deaf, and blind to its environment.

The educational effect of life has been tremendous in its influence on the human character and characteristics of the rising generation, as it always has been and always will be on every generation. One of the best evidences to be found that this effect has been for the most part good in modern youth is the obvious circumstance that to-day's youngsters of both sexes are beginning to doubt the myths, miracle tales, ancient chronicles, and other imperfect and misleading legends which once were called "history" and were used by the shrewd, the unscrupulous, and the fanatical for the exploitation of the ignorant.

In many details, therefore, it is a good thing that the outlook of our modern young people has altered as it has. Indeed I do not happen to think of any detail in which it is bad.

There is no justification for the view that the morals of modern youth are deteriorating. If we take the world as a whole and base our conclusions upon fact instead of upon proclaimed theories, we shall find that the morals of young people are better at the present time than they have ever been before. This is not to deny details of any special conditions which may have risen in particular places and conditions. I know nothing about what may have been the local evidence leading any student of the situation to conclude from what he has seen around him that youth in general is going to the dogs. It may be true in special instances; we always have had to class a certain small proportion of young people with that larger group of older people who have not known how to get the best out of life or what to do with it, and so have done improper things with it and got the worst out of it. In the main, morals of modern youth are better than those of their fathers and grandfathers and much better than those of their remoter ancestors.

I-1927

XXI · THE UNREST OF YOUTH

ONE OF THE many other things about that which we call current thought is that people speak of a "prevailing unrest," applying this term particularly to the mental state of young people. It is not "unrest" in the bad sense in which the word is used which keeps young people moving, thinking, doing. It is, however, the opposite of stagnation and that is a fine thing for the world. The steady increase of activity is mostly orderly, aspiring, and worth-while, having been brought about by those changes in the methods of our lives which can be attributed to new inventions and methods.

The passing generation is likely to give a disagreeable and undeserved significance to the fermentation of new ideas among the young of the present and the coming generations. "Unrest" may be and often has been divine. We shall have no better conditions in the future if we are satisfied with all those which we have at present.

The fact that the young people of to-day, generally speaking, are more intelligent than the young people of 1890, for example, when I, myself, was forty-three years old, is a pretty good guarantee that the young people of thirty-six years in the future will be more intelligent than those of to-day. What young people may be a century from now I do not care to predict, nor do I dare. They will be an improvement on the young people of the present. That is all I feel it safe to say. I am very hopeful of the next generation in America and of the many generations which will follow it.

Of course much will depend on education. There are those who claim that the young person of to-day is overeducated, and that this means arrival of the time when parents and teachers to a greater extent should let youth alone to follow its own initiative.

Perhaps education has changed less than we think. Like religion it is very slow to change. In time, however, new methods will be introduced which will greatly improve it. I do not care to speculate as to just what they will be, but in many details, and, in some essentials, they will differ from those of to-day and the new education, when formulated, will be more effective than any we now know.

I-1927

XXII · MATURITY AND YOUTH

AT PRESENT most young people leave their schools only partially educated, and rapidly forget a large part even of that which they have been taught. I cannot believe that if they had been taught the right things in the right way this would be the case so frequently and notably. They fail to learn because the methods of teaching are wrong. They forget because the methods of instruction have made them actually dislike knowledge. Learning is not made interesting and most young people will not acquire information which seems to be uninteresting. Interest and simplicity should be the keynotes of all education, I believe. It is impossible to fascinate young minds with dull complexities.

I have been asked if I believe that girls and boys should be educated together. I am not very emphatic on this subject, but I think they might better be kept apart during the school studying years. It may be that, together, they distract each other's attention. Whether coeducation always will be unwise is another matter.

Perhaps we have gone too far in various things. I cannot think that the free discussion of whatever subject, in any society, however mixed, which seems to have become a habit among some groups of those who call themselves "the élite," is a good thing. It is a mere stupidity to rob life of all its reservations.

But in spite of all the errors we have made, the young people of to-day are healthier minded than any of the past. And of course this indicates that humanity has been more right than wrong in its influences on youth. Even if this be chargeable to youth itself, as some leaders of the self-dubbed "youth movement" say, the credit must be given to maturity as well, for every general impulse is the result of community, nation, and world thought. Thinking is a cumulative process. The knowledge of to-day is nothing but the sum of the knowledge of the past.

Maturity often is more absurd than youth and very frequently is most unjust to youth.

A wave of accusation sweeps America just now, one of its details being the charge that young people are drinking far too much of alcoholic stimulants. I try to watch life as it passes in review before me (it passes in review before every man, if he but knew it, and it is the most interesting of parades), and nothing I have seen made me aware that youth as a whole is doing anything of the sort. A few morons may be, but it would be a melancholy world if we judged youth as a whole by the morons we may chance to find among young people. We do not call apples a bad fruit because some have blemishes.

The best service which maturity can render youth is to encourage and forward every worthy form of education. I have reason to believe that the systems which at present we have managed to work out, particularly in our colleges, are in many details inefficient, but that they are better than nothing goes without saying. Primary education is an absolute necessity and the higher education, so called, should have every encouragement, I think. Only by giving it as much thought and labor as we can devote to it can we bring about in it those improvements which so obviously are necessary.

I have been frequently asked if my questionnaire system of grading youth has proved worthwhile. A good deal of nonsense has been written about those questionnaires. Any man who is working with any sort of material and depending for his success on the intelligence with which he selects and handles it is stupid if he does not use every possible method of ascertaining as many facts as possible pertaining to it. Mere looking at a young man who is applying for employment can tell you nothing about him except that he is high grade or low grade as the case may be.

An employer needs to know far more than that. He must have certain details if he wishes to avoid waste of time in efforts to train human material which cannot be trained. The human mind cannot be analyzed as the piece of metal can be, but a good deal can be learned about it by finding out, first, whether or not it is really a thinking and remembering machine. An employee who has a good memory will be of far greater value to an employer than one who has not. And so the questionnaires were valuable as memory tests, which was all the public and the men who wrote about them seemed to think it possible that they could be.

But they were far more than that. Framed with the object of bringing out many things of value which were not apparent to the man who examined them casually they rendered me good service. Mental capacity, attentiveness, quickness, and accuracy or their opposites may be indicated in the answers to a questionnaire and, further, it is possible to devise a list of queries which will draw out of the person answering them much evidence as to character in its various important manifestations. Just why there should have been so much excitement because I, an employer, decided to use questionnaires in an effort to determine whether or not applicants for positions were fit to fill them always has puzzled me. Every school and college in the world depends upon examinations as virtually its only means of establishing pupils' fitness or unfitness for promotion.

But there was nothing in the results of my experimental application of the questionnaire idea to discourage me about modern youth, although there may have been something in the comment upon those results to discourage me with regard to modern maturity. If my questionnaires revealed to me any details of inefficiency in our educational processes surely that knowledge is valuable to me as an employer. The questionnaires served their purpose. They were devised with the idea that they might increase my efficiency as the head of a business enterprise, for the first requisite of business success is ability to select intelligently the people to be employed.

The mere fact that I am now convinced that college training should be encouraged proves that I make no attack on it. If I am convinced that, being inefficient in some details, it can be very much improved, I also am convinced that most other human processes as carried on to-day can and will be very much improved in days to come. The fact which I have mentioned that young people of this generation are healthier-minded than those who preceded them is and must be an outcome of the education they have had, whether they have acquired it in primary schools, or colleges, in their homes, through reading books, through studying the newspapers, or in whatever way.

What is a college? An institute of learning. What is a business? An institute of learning. Life, itself, is an institute of learning.

I-1927

XXIII · EMPLOYMENT AND EDUCATION

ATROPHY OF perception afflicts America today. The eye sees, but no message goes from it to the brain. Despite unquestioned vision of the fact, there is no sensing of it by the individual before whom it is placed. It is seen physically but not mentally.

I have been asked about the effectiveness of my questionnaire of grading youth, and although much fault has been found with it by those who do not understand it, I would say it is unqualifiedly effective. I always welcome criticism. It helps me think and often shows me where I have been wrong. In this instance it has shown me where I have been absolutely right.

We still hear a good deal about the questionnaires which we request those applying for executive and other high class jobs with us to answer. Some condemn, and a very few applaud. We know now that the plan is right.

The questionnaire idea grew out of my desire for a way other than sheer, bullhead luck of finding good men for the jobs we offer. Competent men in our jobs mean success for us; incompetent men in them would mean failure.

Before I worked out the plan I had to decide on the one quality most important to us. Studying over this, I was forced to the decision that the best of qualifications is a fine memory.

Every intelligent man reads much; words intended to convey information pass before his eyes, even if he does not study as the college student is supposed to study.

But information which merely passes before a man's eyes does not help him unless, in passing, it is impressed upon his memory and stored there, where he not only can but automatically will get it at a second's notice when it is required.

I had known this for many years. But I had had a hard time finding the men with such memories, because there had been no means of testing them except by putting them to work. Reflection upon this brought the idea of the questionnaires, and I drew them up believing they would select for me from among the ruck of applicants the possessors of comprehending and retentive minds.

The subject matter of the questions I regarded and

still regard as unimportant; they were designed not to test information but the ability to retain it. I knew that every college man—and these examinations were given to none but college men—had been required to learn the answers to every question on the list. The point was: Had his mind preserved and kept available for instant use the facts which had passed into it?

I never before was so shocked and astonished as I was by the results. They proved to me that something is radically wrong in the way we in the United States are training minds.

It is obvious that our schools and colleges are benefiting but a small proportion of those going to them. The experiment makes revelations with regard to American education which are not less than appalling, with the college making a far better showing than the lower schools, although it is quite clear that even colleges and technical institutions are far from what we fondly have been hoping them to be. The lower schools' results seem to be tragic. One man graduated from the public schools of Yonkers could not answer any query on the short and simple list.

Among my violent critics have been, of course, the men responsible for our primary and secondary education. In general, their claim is that boys and young men go to them not to learn but to learn how to learn.

It seems that youth is no longer expected to acquire

knowledge through education, but through education to acquire the ability to acquire knowledge out of the processes of life surrounding him after the ending of school days.

According to certain college Presidents, the education which their institutions offer trains young men to find the books in which is noted down the knowledge which they will require in later life to suit their practical purposes and serve their aesthetic tastes.

It is a far more serious matter that those who shape our lower schools should take a similar view, for it implies that the place for facts is in the books, not in the brain, and that the function of the brain is to know how to get facts out of books when facts may be required. Personally I hold the brain above the book.

Perhaps the failure of the colleges lies principally in their lack of appreciation of the dull inferiority of the material which the lower schools deliver to them; it may be because of this that they do not go down the line to help toward the correction of a national evil.

"The colleges do not take men to teach them isolated facts," was the indignant statement of one man who thought I had attacked the colleges.

If this be true then the colleges are wrong, for young men cannot think efficiently unless they have facts in their minds ready to serve as bases for their thinking. It would be a melancholy world if all experts had to fly to libraries every time they were required to pass on anything.

Certainly the brains should have the facts. If a brain possesses an enormous number of facts, those facts, through action of the subconscious mind, will automatically keep themselves available when needed and will automatically keep themselves out of the way, not interfering when not required.

The employer who does not study and judge men before hiring them is foolish. There is no way whereby men may be judged save by finding out how much and what they know, and especially their capacity for learning—memory. Men cannot be judged rightly by looks. I have tried it and been fooled many times. Possession or non-possession of great quantities of facts has slight, if any, influence upon appearance.

The questionnaires which I devised asked nothing which the average young college graduate seeking a position in a great industrial plant ought not to know, for they required no information concerning anything not in the college or school courses. For example, I used the first words of the Æneid. Almost none identified them.

That revealed the fact that the memory of the examined men did not retain facts which their minds certainly had studied. This was the important point. I tried to make a mind test. The mind which would retain facts studied in the college would retain facts brought to its attention in later business life and vice versa.

In mechanical engineering I put the simplest problems, such as: Suppose so-and-so does so-and-so, what then? Very few could answer.

That was another serious revelation. Young college men found themselves unable to suppose. They had no imagination. And many failed in memory, for, trained in colleges and technical schools, they revealed ignorance of the first rules of mechanics.

But again I must explain that those who have not had such training make even worse results upon examination. The fault unquestionably lies further down the line than the colleges.

I am all for the college men. They are the best we have, but they might be a great deal better, for only 7 per cent of the total we examined answered our very simple questions with evidence of decent memory and actual intelligence.

The fact is that our youth, bright though they may be as children, are not educated so as to take college training with 100 per cent benefit; they do not get the preliminary training necessary to the development of a reasonable fitness in college for the ultimate of usefulness in later life.

They are not started right. Whether or not the colleges would do well with them if they went to them as good material, they are spoiled long before they get to college. I don't know the way out of this tragic difficulty. If I did I'd do my best to get it generally adopted.

Perhaps that which we need may lie along the lines of visual education. Experience with the tests seems to favor a theory which I experimented with when I first became interested in motion pictures; I thought the film would be the most effective instrument of education. I began work on a complete set of educational films, but fire destroyed them and I never rebegan the task.

Perhaps the Government may have to make such films before we really learn how to teach our youth. The atrophy, the paralysis of curiosity, the ending of the power to observe, seems to begin between the ages of eleven and fifteen. Perhaps if a boy can be kept interested till he's twenty-one he won't become a victim.

Whatever may be the remedy, the situation is one to shock the pride of an American. I have in my possession proofs of this; I have the proofs but find my national spirit in revolt against their truth. The time surely has come for us to stop, look and listen.

Those who sneer at our experiments do not understand the sort of citizenship we are getting; they do not realize that our American material is now deteriorating; nor do they understand that if we would retain supremacy in modern manufacturing we must have fewer goats, more sheep and some process of eliminating goats before they get into the sheepfold. We've got to raise our average.

I have made up my mind that when a man under the present system, not started right, reaches the age of twenty-one he's through. Atrophy of his intelligence has started. Apparently, as a matter of fact, it may begin earlier—at, say eleven.

Atrophy means shrinkage, withering, due to lack of proper exercise, and there are no corrective processes.

The young man whose mind has been allowed to atrophy through lack of definite, continuous, hard work has few possibilities or none. His time has passed. He's through before he starts.

Two chaps start even. One does and one does not feel interested in life, the difference between them always being due, if they really started even, to training at home or school. The interested one, even though ill-equipped to start with, can acquire intelligence, and the other, though otherwise far more fortunate, will be helpless, fixed for life; his brain will be atrophied. Nothing new will stick to him. Of this I have made sure through wide experimentation.

Thousands of the atrophied cumber American industry.

Such men, of course, cannot see whether work is right or wrong. They make bad foremen. There are thousands of them—well meaning, doubtless, but entirely hopeless. It's atrophy—atrophy of the connection between the eye and the brain. The eyes perceive, but the brain does not get a message from them.

When a good man reaches an opinion he probably employs in the process at least a hundred times as many facts as he himself would think possible. This is very notably true in business.

It is very largely memory. I believe the men who have shaped our big businesses almost invariably have had splendid memories.

But here it is important to explain that such memories as I refer to should not be expected of men far past maturity. The man of, say, forty-five to sixty has specialized.

But youngsters fresh from the schools and without fine memories, are starting life with brain-machinery either bad at the beginning or damaged by our educational processes. They are our penalty for making our schools dull. Out of school the unimportant is made interesting; if the important is not interesting in school then the unimportant will win the attention of the young. Our youth stores its mind with that which it finds most interesting.

Perhaps only about 6 per cent of the newspapers of the country took me seriously when I started on this work. The comments were various. The Literary Digest said I must be wrong because I asked for isolated facts. I had to laugh, for the Literary Digest is made up of isolated facts. Its mighty value lies in its determination to survey widely. It criticized me for demanding in the human mind that which it supplies in each one of its issues.

The trouble is in education, not in the American mind. Our little children are all right. I tried some out by having made a special film worked out partly in a kitchen and partly in a laboratory by a little boy and little girl, their procedure actually comprising a brief but not too simple lesson in chemistry. The mothers of my little guests agreed to write out for me what the little ones reported after they reached home.

I was amazed at their reports. The experiment fully showed that the child from eight to ten years old may be made by visual instruction to understand quite complicated scientific phenomena which certainly the printed word and the recited lesson never could make clear to them. One shows something being done, the other tells in strings of words how it is done.

An intelligent man in Baton Rouge had been born blind. Suddenly he received his sight. He could not differentiate between a circle and a ball, although he had felt of them many times in his blind years and had had them described to him. There is a tip for educators. Untrained eyes did not send to the brain the facts concerning that on which they look. We must be careful not to breed a race with untrained eyes. It would not have hands superlatively trained as this man had.

One hundred per cent functioning is not impossible to human beings. Don't let any one make you believe it is.

I have no theories to advance with regard to the means of education most likely to preserve us from the early mental atrophy which certainly now threatens us. I have only facts—the facts of the existence of the peril.

My regret is that in the United States each year the colleges turn out only 185,000 graduates, far too few to furnish one-twelfth of the men required each year to fill industrial positions calling for mentally trained men. And many, perhaps most, of all these graduates seek professional careers. The shortage of the trained among our industries would be tragic even if all trained men were well trained.

To-day there is far more reason for the possession of many facts than there ever was before. Industry continually becomes more complex.

The schools must change, the colleges must change and, more than all, home life and parental relationships with children certainly must change or serious national harm inevitably will result.

It is the people's business. Thousands of things to-day cannot get to the public—things the public needs. I mean—because their production is in the hands of the incompetent, who alone are now available for factory work.

Many a manufacturer, through inability to get

good foremen, finds it impossible to introduce improvements which greatly would reduce his product's cost. An old machine, for instance, will make 200 parts per hour with a net loss of two. A new one is created to make 1,000 parts per hour. But the best operatives available run it so badly that it wastes 300 of the thousand parts; this increased waste makes its use impossible. It is due to the low grade intelligence of the operative. He is not as good as the machine. He is not an A man.

The situation is alarming. America to-day does not produce ability in unlimited quantities, developing in accordance with the opportunities the Nation offers. There is far more opportunity than there is ability—and that means bad things for America.

My real feeling with regard to colleges is that while they do not deserve all the condemnation I have been credited with heaping on them, yet they measurably fail. Careful thought convinces me that this is because the men who run them never have been out in the great world of struggle. Professors, usually, are men untried in any sort of competition comparable with that which their students eventually must face. Often their fathers and grandfathers never have been tested.

Speaking generally, such men cannot impart the right ideas to the boys, for they themselves are ignorant.

The general application of the questionnaire plan

might be a good thing for the country. Explorations outside the group of job-seekers produce paralyzing evidence. Many now ranked as highly competent, even as distinguished, would show up badly after a very simple 300-word questionnaire.

VII-31-1921

XXIV · THE WILL TO WORK

MODERN COLLEGES are not what they should be. I do not approve of the present-day college graduate, for as a rule the right kind of men don't go to college. Take the average college man, his knowledge of his surroundings and environment is usually inadequate. What young men need is a broad general understanding of every little thing in life, such as would fit them to be able to answer my questionnaire.

The main objection that I have against a college graduate is that he objects to work, especially if it is dirty. He does not want a job with much work to it, and when he does get a position, he expects to be appointed foreman at the end of the sixth week. Most of the men working for me have never gone to college. Those college graduates that I have usually show a lack of imagination. They scarcely have any suggestions to make in their daily routine which might lead to improvements in their various departments.

College is a good place for the man who wants to

work, but unfortunately there are very few of this type nowadays. Yet if a man wants to succeed, it is not a necessity that he should get his education at college. If he is to amount to anything, he will broaden himself out without the need of college training. What we need in America are more men with technical training since we are a commercial country by nature. We have enough lawyers, doctors and literary men. There are plenty of openings for ambitious men in this country. Why is it that we have so few $10,000 a year men? It is not that there is a lack of such positions, but rather that there is a scarcity of men of sufficient caliber to fill these openings.

"Everyone in this world sets his own salary," is my slogan, and I defy any man to prove the opposite. I have found out that whatever a man is during the first six weeks after he gets a job, he will be the same after 60 years and no amount of advice will have any effect whatsoever in changing him. When he is 21 years of age, he is set for life and if a dullard then he will continue so through life. The main quality for success in my estimation is ambition with a will for work.

XI-17-1922

XXV · THE COLLEGE OF BUSINESS

BUSINESS IS A college more exacting than any of the schools and universities which make up what we call our educational system. Its courses are strictly practical and its teachers are what men of this generation describe by the term "hard boiled," but it is a school, a college, or a university as the student of its compulsory education may elect. Its courses are not always free. For some of the instruction all of us pay very high tuition. Only to a certain extent are they elective. That only a small percentage of the young men of to-day adapt themselves effectively to such of them as they choose and pass their examinations for promotion with high standing, is sufficient indication that general preparation for their requirements is far from ideal. That is where there is the greatest room for real improvement in our education. When we consider it as an actual preparation for the hard, cold, delightful, warm, inevitable experiences of actual life we shall have developed it to just about its limit.

To say that our educators need education is merely to say of them what they are constantly proclaiming of themselves and everybody else in their own speeches. They know it and most of them are trying earnestly to get the education that they need.

But it probably remains true that the proportion of so-called success in business is smaller than the proportion of so-called success in education, that is, that a greater percentage of the boys and girls who go to college meet the requirements of their colleges as crystallized in their final examinations than, later, meet the final requirements of success when the same boys and girls go into business or any manner of mature activity. This is most important, for the later success means usefulness and happiness.

One reason for this, and of course there are many reasons other than defects in educational methods, although these undoubtedly are of great importance, is that something untoward seems to happen to domestic life in many instances. It is not good for man— or woman, either—to live alone. Of that I am sure.

And one tendency of the times which I am inclined to think is bad is the apparently increasing avoidance of marriage or its postponement until an age when the adaptation of one individual of the couple involved to the other is difficult because habits have been fixed so firmly that their adjustment is a difficult or at least an annoying process. Obviously, therefore, it seems to me, early marriages should be encouraged.

We are getting knowledge from many sources which used not to be available, however, and this will help us solve all problems.

Life, itself, without the assistance of colleges and universities, is becoming an advanced institution of learning. This may be truer in the fields of material science than in some others; it certainly is true there. Radio and other things are popularizing scientific knowledge. It is not improbable that the aggregate of such information acquired by youths during the past twelve months as the result of their interest in radio is greater than the aggregate acquired by youths during the same period as the result of study in the schools and colleges. There is no way of determining this, but it is certain that even crude experimentation by youth with the making and use of scientific instruments and appliances, with the combination of chemicals, and with such hints of the unseen forces as are certain to result from effort of this sort, is highly educational. Radio is popularizing science among the young and that is something which the schools, necessarily, have frequently failed to do because of the mistaken mental attitude which has been forced on youth concerning schools, the belief that something disagreeable inevitably must be connected with the getting of scholastic education.

Perhaps that may be the fundamental error of our educational efforts up to date. I do not know. I am not an educational expert and can only guess with regard to a matter which has been, the world over, left too much to guesswork. The young college men who fail to pass the general intelligence test demanded by a questionnaire very likely may not be deficient in fundamental intelligence; their failure to acquire and later on to be able to summon instantaneously to their aid useful knowledge, and their apparent lack of that power of ordered reasoning which should be the most important of education's fruits, may be due to imperfections in the methods chosen by their elders for the dissemination of knowledge.

In fact, I think this usually may be the case. But I am positive that non-scholastic study of any scientific subject such as recently has been given to radio by our young people is a great good fortune to a nation. These things definitely increase the habit of thinking scientifically.

Electricity in its various manifestations, the steam-engine and railroad, and to an even greater degree the internal combustion engine and its child, the automobile, have had a great developing effect upon the minds of youth. Radio now serves a similar purpose. Whether the airplane and flying will have a comparable general effect I doubt. Children will not get accustomed to flight as they have become accustomed to automobiling. Many years must elapse, I think, before airplanes will be so developed that they can come into general use as motor-cars have. The present types of flying machines have their utility, but only in the hands of experts.

I-1927

XXVI · VISUAL EDUCATION

MOTION PICTURES can be applied to a scientific, systematic course of memory training in the schools, taking the children at an early age when the mind is plastic enough to adapt itself most readily to new habits of thought.

Most of our textbooks fail on two big counts. They are not sufficiently human, and their application is not sufficiently practical. Their tendency seems to be to look upon the whole process of education as a job of dull and uninteresting work—with the apparent argument that the duller and more uninteresting it is made the more credit there is for doing it.

When we have tried to change that viewpoint we have used too much sugar coating, and have applied too many fanciful "isms," and have gone to the opposite extreme. Education isn't play—and it can't be made to look like play. It is hard, hard work. But it can be made interesting work.

Suppose we try the illustration of mathematics. Show the average boy a textbook on arithmetic, and he will back away from it as from a woodpile that needs chopping when he wants to go fishing. Show it to the average man, and it will conjure up visions of long, weary hours and splitting headaches that it meant for him as a youngster.

The reason is that we have not tried to make arithmetic interesting. What could visual education do to remedy this? It might show us how to apply arithmetic to life.

For a concrete object lesson we might exhibit a motion picture of electricity as the world's great burden-bearer, relating particularly to incandescent lighting. I am picking this as an illustration because I happen to know more about electric lighting than most other subjects. Hundreds of other subjects, of course, will suggest themselves, and would do as well.

Our film might show one of our modern central power plants, with its giant dynamos and turbines, its atmosphere of driving energy, and its network of wires stretching out to the four points of the compass to carry the unseen power from the place where it is generated to the multitudinous places where it is used.

Our first purpose is psychological—to eliminate the student's sense of petty classroom drudgery. Our next purpose is more practical—to carry him into the realities of the world's work, and to make him a personal part of it. If we can do this we have made a great forward step right at the start.

Our visual arithmetic lesson begins with a comparatively simple problem—our pictures changing, of course, as we go along. American power plants now serve 9,500,000 homes. The estimated number of homes in the United States is 21,000,000. What percentage receives electric power?

From our power plant we might continue with scenes at a great lamp factory producing the globes for the electric current. Let's see what we could do for our arithmetic lesson with such a background.

It needs about 280,000,000 tungsten lamps each year to supply the market to-day. And yet the first lamp factory in the world—the Edison Lamp Works, now located at Harrison, N. J.—was not started until 1880, and I was told it would never pay. The output for our first year was about 25,000 globes. How many times that figure would be required for the present market?

If each lamp measures an average of five inches in length, and they were placed end to end, how many times across the Atlantic Ocean from New York to Liverpool would they reach?

A household using twenty-one lamps requires about seven new lamps each year. What percentage is this? If these lamps had been bought at the retail prices of the first year of the lamp factory, they would have cost $1.25 each. How much would the family save by the decreased prices of to-day?

In all of the above no effort has been made to divide mathematics into any formal sections such as addition, subtraction, multiplication, and division. All of those, of course, could be worked out in detail along systematic lines.

Now let us take the class in geography. It seems to me that motion pictures offer here a rather astonishing substitute for the colorless, standardized lessons of the textbooks—not only an opportunity to teach directly from a busy world at work but with all of the atmosphere of adventure, romance, achievement.

We could teach history, of course, in much the same way, and literature, and biology—and in our advanced courses chemistry, geology, physics. There is no limitation to the camera. It is simply a matter of the right direction.

II-21-1925

V
The Philosophy of Paine

THE PHILOSOPHY OF PAINE

XXVII

TOM PAINE has almost no influence on present-day thinking in the United States because he is unknown to the average citizen. Perhaps I might say right here that this is a national loss and a deplorable lack of understanding concerning the man who first proposed and first wrote those impressive words, 'the United States of America.' But it is hardly strange. Paine's teachings have been debarred from schools everywhere and his views of life misrepresented until his memory is hidden in shadows, or he is looked upon as of unsound mind.

We never had a sounder intelligence in this Republic. He was the equal of Washington in making American liberty possible. Where Washington performed Paine devised and wrote. The deeds of one in the field were matched by the deeds of the other with his pen. Washington himself appreciated Paine at his true worth. Franklin knew him for a great patriot and clear thinker. He was a friend and confidant of Jefferson, and the two must often have debated the academic and practical phases of liberty.

I consider Paine our greatest political thinker. As

we have not advanced, and perhaps never shall advance, beyond the Declaration and Constitution, so Paine has had no successors who extended his principles. Although the present generation knows little of Paine's writings, and although he has almost no influence upon contemporary thought, Americans of the future will justly appraise his work. I am certain of it. Truth is governed by natural laws and cannot be denied. Paine spoke truth with a peculiarly clear and forceful ring. Therefore time must balance the scales. The Declaration and the Constitution expressed in form Paine's theory of political rights. He worked in Philadelphia at the time that the first document was written, and occupied a position of intimate contact with the nation's leaders when they framed the Constitution.

Certainly we may believe that Washington had a considerable voice in the Constitution. We know that Jefferson had much to do with the document. Franklin also had a hand and probably was responsible in even larger measure for the Declaration. But all of these men had communed with Paine. Their views were intimately understood and closely correlated. There is no doubt whatever that the two great documents of American liberty reflect the philosophy of Paine.

We may look in other directions, where the trace is plainer, easier definitely to establish, for evidences of his influence. Paine, you know, came over to the

Colonies after meeting Franklin in London. He had encountered numerous misfortunes, and Franklin gave him letters to friends back home which resulted in his becoming editor of the Pennsylvania Magazine in January of 1775. It is highly interesting that circumstance should have brought him to America at that time and placed him in such a position. Paine had little education, in the school sense of the term, but he had read avidly and written a great deal before meeting Franklin. Once placed at the editor's desk of a new American periodical, he found time and opportunity exactly suited to his spirit and his genius.

The Pennsylvania Magazine began to bristle—so much so that its owner, and the cooler heads of Philadelphia, were worried by Paine's writings. Looking back to those times we cannot, without much reading, clearly gauge the sentiment of the Colonies. Perhaps the larger number of responsible men still hoped for peace with England. They did not even venture to express the matter that way. Few men, indeed, had thought in terms of war.

Then Paine wrote 'Common Sense,' an anonymous tract which immediately stirred the fires of liberty. It flashed from hand to hand throughout the Colonies. One copy reached the New York Assembly, in session at Albany, and a night meeting was voted to answer this unknown writer with his clarion call to liberty. The Assembly met, but could find no suitable answer. Tom Paine had inscribed a document which never has been answered adversely, and never can be, so long as man esteems his priceless possession.

In 'Common Sense' Paine flared forth with a document so powerful that the Revolution became inevitable. Washington recognized the difference, and in his calm way said that matters never could be the same again. It must be remembered that 'Common Sense' preceded the Declaration and affirmed the very principles that went into the national doctrine of liberty. But that affirmation was made with more vigor, more of the fire of the patriot and was exactly suited to the hour. It is probable that we should have had the Revolution without Tom Paine. Certainly it could not be forestalled, once he had spoken.

I have always been interested in this man. My father had a set of Tom Paine's books on the shelf at home. I must have opened the covers about the time I was 13. And I can still remember the flash of enlightenment which shone from his pages. It was a revelation, indeed, to encounter his views on political and religious matters, so different from the views of many people around us. Of course I did not understand him very well, but his sincerity and ardor made an impression upon me that nothing has ever served to lessen.

I have heard it said that Paine borrowed from Montesquieu and Rousseau. Maybe he had read them both and learned something from each. I do not know. But I doubt that Paine ever bororwed a line from any man. Perhaps he gained strength from the fact that the springs of his wisdom lay within himself, and he spoke so clearly because the man's spirit yearned to reach other spirits.

Many a person who could not comprehend Rousseau, and would be puzzled by Montesquieu, could understand Paine as an open book. He wrote with a clarity, a sharpness of outline and exactness of speech that even a schoolboy should be able to grasp. There is nothing false, little that is subtle, and an impressive lack of the negative in Paine. He literally cried to his reader for a comprehending hour, and then filled that hour with such sagacious reasoning as we find surpassed nowhere else in American letters—seldom in any school of writing.

Paine would have been the last to look upon himself as a man of letters. Liberty was the dear companion of his heart; truth in all things his object. Yet he has left us such stirring lines as those of 'The Crisis,' where he says: 'These are the times that try men's souls. . . . Tyranny, like hell, is not easily conquered.' Even an unappreciative posterity knows that line, but we, perhaps, remember him best for his declaration: 'The world is my country; to do good my religion.'

Again we see the spontaneous genius at work in "The Rights of Man," and that genius busy at his favorite task—liberty. Written hurriedly and in the heat of controversy, "The Rights of Man" yet compares favorably with classical models, and in some places rises to vaulting heights. Its appearance outmatched events attending Burke's effort in his "Reflections."

Instantly the English public caught hold of this new contribution. It was more than a defense of liberty; it was a world declaration of what Paine had declared before in the Colonies. His reasoning was so cogent, his command of the subject so broad, that his legion of enemies found it hard to answer him. "Tom Paine is quite right," said Pitt, the Prime Minister, "but if I were to encourage his views we should have a bloody revolution."

Here we see the progressive quality of Paine's genius at its best. "The Rights of Man" amplified and reasserted what already had been said in "Common Sense," with now a greater force and the power of a maturing mind. Just when Paine was at the height of his renown, an indictment for treason confronted him. About the same time he was elected a member of the Revolutionary Assembly and escaped to France.

So little did he know of the French tongue that addresses to his constituents had to be translated by an interpreter. But he sat in the assembly. Shrinking from the guillotine, he encountered Robespierre's enmity, and presently found himself in prison, facing that dread instrument.

But his imprisonment was fertile. Already he had written the first part of "The Age of Reason" and now turned his time to the latter part. Presently his second escape cheated Robespierre of vengeance, and in the course of events "The Age of Reason" appeared. Instantly it became a source of contention which still endures. Paine returned to the United States a little broken, and went to live at his home in New Rochelle —a public gift. Many of his old companions in the struggle for liberty avoided him, and he was publicly condemned by the unthinking.

Paine suffered then, as now he suffers not so much because of what he wrote as from the misinterpretations of others. He has been called an atheist, but atheist he was not. Paine believed in a supreme intelligence, as representing the idea which other men often express by the name of deity.

His Bible was the open face of nature, the broad skies, the green hills. He disbelieved the ancient myths and miracles taught by established creeds. But the attacks on those creeds—or on persons devoted to them —have served to darken his memory, casting a shadow across the closing years of his life.

When Theodore Roosevelt termed Tom Paine a dirty little atheist he surely spoke from lack of understanding. It was a stricture, an inaccurate charge of the sort that has dimmed the greatness of this eminent American. But the true measure of his stature will yet be appreciated. The torch which he handed on will not be extinguished. If Paine had ceased his writings with "The Rights of Man" he would have been hailed today as one of the two or three outstanding figures of the Revolution. But "The Age of Reason" cost him glory at the hands of his countrymen—a greater loss to them than to Tom Paine.

I was always interested in Paine the inventor. He conceived and designed the iron bridge and the hollow candle; the principle of the modern central draught burner. The man had a sort of universal genius. He was interested in a diversity of things; but his special creed, his first thought, was liberty.

Traducers have said that he spent his last days drinking in pothouses. They have pictured him as a wicked old man coming to a sorry end. But I am persuaded that Paine must have looked with magnanimity and sorrow on the attacks of his countrymen. That those attacks have continued down to our day, with scarcely any abatement, is an indication of how strong prejudice, when once aroused, may become. It has been a custom in some quarters to hold up Paine as an example of everything bad.

The memory of Tom Paine will outlive all this. No man who helped to lay the foundations of our liberty —who stepped forth as the champion of so difficult a cause—can be permanently obscured by such attacks. Tom Paine should be read by his countrymen. I commend his fame to their hands.

VI-7-1925

VI
Man and Machine

MAN AND MACHINE

XXVIII

I DO NOT BELIEVE the Government should do anything but regulate the activities of its people, give them a free swing, and see that every man is protected in that which he produces. A department of inventions is not wanted. What is wanted is that the methods of court procedure be changed and the courts realize that the man who makes inventions, by the very nature of things, cannot be a business man, familiar with its merciless code; and they should take this into consideration and protect him.

Economic questions involve thousands of complicated factors which contribute to a certain result. It takes a lot of brain power and a lot of scientific data to solve these questions. In the first place, they ought to be studied scientifically, the same way we go about discovering the so-called secrets of nature.

When I want to discover something, I begin by reading up everything that has been done along that line in the past—that's what all these books in the library are for. I see what has been accomplished at great labor and expense in the past. I gather the data of many thousands of experiments as a starting point, and then I make thousands more. On this money question we ought to go back several hundred years before the Roman era and find out all about the financial systems and their results from that time to this. Then we would know something to build upon. Take the tariff question. An item is put in a bill and it is expected to produce tremendous results. The actual result is just nothing. But another item, small and unconsidered, produces enormous changes in the national economy. What do the legislators know about that?

Herbert Spencer had the right idea. He took thirty-two acts of Parliament and had them traced down and found that twenty-nine produced exactly the contrary effect to the effect intended. Spencer had the right scientific idea of investigating economics. He hired thirty clerks to run down those laws and see what their results were.

There are plenty of wrong things in our society. Everything is for show; the newspapers make a show of everything. Things are wrong at the top and at the bottom. Between the two they are fairly tolerable. There isn't too much happiness floating around, and the man who gets nearest his rightful share of it has a character, a little bungalow in the country, and a family. What does the very rich man get? He's always scheming, always suspicious of the men around him. His money is mostly out, invested. Yes, he lives in a fine house, rides in an automobile, and he eats three meals a day when he feels able to. I defy any one to prove that he gets much out of life. Money doesn't make a man happy and it doesn't make a man a good companion.

Things are wrong enough, and to right them we need two remedies. One is to develop the convolutions in man's brain, those coils inside with which he does his thinking. We have gradually developed what we have in there, and if we could develop about two convolutions more we would be able to grasp and solve our social problems. The other remedy is education. Education of the right sort in early childhood. You can't do anything with a grown man. You can't do anything or predict anything about a woman, either, because she is all instinct and emotion. But take a child four years old and its mind is plastic, and whatever you put in there will always stay. Teach a child of four that the moon is made of green cheese, and tho you give him a thorough scientific education afterward there will always be, at the bottom of his mind, a feeling that the moon is somehow possibly made of green cheese. See how religious beliefs implanted in childhood stay with the adult in spite of everything. It is necessary to take them young and to teach morality and character, to fix ideas in those plastic minds so that it will be impossible for them to think wrong or do wrong. What we want to do in this world is to eradicate the crooks, high and low, and to do that we must begin early and prevent them from going crooked at the start.

Yes, I know the Socialist viewpoint. I guess the reason for their belief is that they see so much fraud everywhere; they get the seamy side of everything. It's a recommendation, of course, for Socialism that there are so many of the intellectual class who sympathize with it or believe in it. But they'll have to improve their ideas to make them practical. So far Russia is the most socialistic country and everything there is like a machine and nobody likes it. They have it in the factories, where, as I saw it in a comic paper over there, they prescribe how many steps to the right and left a workingman takes at the noon hour in going from the factory door to his eating place. They have it in the schools, forcing all kinds of dry stuff into the heads of school children. Learning ought to be made easy and pleasant. It can be done with the aid of moving pictures. I could tell any one a great deal about a dynamo and it would be hard for him to understand; but I could show everything in a few pictures so that a child would understand—and would never forget.

Now, the Socialists, if they amount to anything, must improve their program—or what is generally accepted as their program. They can't hope to reduce all mankind to a dead level. They can't figure to abolish capital, which is the accumulated results of labor, mental and physical, of all the ages, and is called wealth, wealth of all the ages. They can't ignore the men who do the thinking and the guiding, the great executive minds to whom society owes most of what it has. Two men start two factories, with the same resources, on opposite sides of the street. One goes bankrupt, the other succeeds. Are those men equal? Or here is a man who goes into a shipyard and without increasing the hours of labor or making any one work harder, manages it so that three ships instead of two are built in a year. This he has done without calling for any more exertion on the part of the men and without increasing their number. Didn't he create extra value and isn't he entitled to extra reward? Such men are not in the class of parasites or market manipulators or stock jugglers. Socialism, if it ever arrives, must provide unlimited incentive for its executive minds and its creators. Unlimited incentive. The motive that I have for inventing is, I guess, like the motive of the billiard player, who always wants to do a little better—to add to his record. Under present conditions I use the reasonable profit which I derive from one invention to make experiments looking toward another invention. If socialism gave me the means to continue inventing, I would invent; but if it failed to do so, or began to tie me down, I would quit.

Machinery has changed things in our society and it will change them a great deal more. The man and the machine act and interact. The time is coming when the machine will do all the work and man will just set it to work. We will feed the raw material in one end and will see our shoes, clothes and everything else we need come out of the other end. The general use of such automatic machinery will be forced by the tactics of radical labor, and at first the working people will suffer, but in the end they will be benefited.

1-5-1914

XXIX · THEY WON'T THINK

EVERY MAN has some forte, something he can do better than he can do anything else. Many men, however, never find the job they are best suited for. And often this is because they do not think enough. Too many men drift lazily into any job, suited or unsuited for them; and when they don't get along well they blame everybody and everything but themselves.

Grouches are nearly always pinheads, small men who have never made any effort to improve their mental capacity.

The brain can be developed just the same as the muscles can be developed, if one will only take the pains to train the mind to think.

Why do so many men never amount to anything? Because they don't think.

I am going to have a sign put up all over my plant, reading "There is no expedient to which a man will not resort to avoid the real labor of thinking." *

---

* This quotation from Sir Joshua Reynolds was hung in every room of Edison's laboratory. It still hangs in a prominent place in his library.

That is true. There is hardly a day that I do not discover how painfully true it is.

What progress individuals could make, and what progress the world would make, if thinking were given proper consideration! It seems to me that not one man in a thousand appreciates what can be accomplished by training the mind to think.

It is because they do not use their thinking powers that so many people have never developed a creditable mentality. The brain that isn't used rusts. The brain that is used responds. The brain is exactly like any other part of the body: it can be strengthened by proper exercise, by proper use. Put your arm in a sling and keep it there for a considerable length of time, and, when you take it out, you find that you can't use it. In the same way, the brain that isn't used suffers atrophy.

By developing your thinking powers you expand the capacity of your brain and attain new abilities. For example, the average person's brain does not observe a thousandth part of what the eye observes. The average brain simply fails to register the things which come before the eye. It is almost incredible how poor our powers of observation—genuine observation—are.

Let me give an illustration: When we first started the incandescent lighting system we had a lamp factory at the bottom of a hill, at Menlo Park. It was a very busy time for us all. Seventy-five of us worked twenty hours every day and slept only four hours—and thrived on it.

I fed them all, and I had a man play an organ all the time we were at work. One midnight, while at lunch, a matter came up which caused me to refer to a cherry tree beside the hill leading from the main works to the lamp factory. Nobody seemed to know anything about the location of the cherry tree. This made me conduct a little investigation, and I found that although twenty-seven of these men had used this path every day for six months not one of them had ever noticed the tree.

The eye sees a great many things, but the average brain records very few of them. Indeed, nobody has the slightest conception of how little the brain 'sees' unless it has been highly trained. I remember dropping in to see a man whose duty was to watch the working of a hundred machines on a table. I asked him if everything was all right.

Yes, everything is all right, he said.

But I had already noticed that two of the machines had stopped. I drew his attention to them, and he was mortified. He confessed that, although his sole duty was to watch and see that every machine was working, he had not noticed that these two had stopped. I could hie myself off and keep busy at thinking forever. I don't need anybody to amuse me. It is the same way with my friends John Burroughs, the naturalist, and Henry Ford, who is a natural-born mechanic. We can derive the most satisfying kind of joy from thinking and thinking and thinking.

The man who doesn't make up his mind to cultivate the habit of thinking misses the greatest pleasure in life. He not only misses the greatest pleasure, but he cannot make the most of himself. All progress, all success, springs from thinking.

Of course, even the most concentrated thinking cannot solve every new problem that the brain can conceive. It usually takes me from five to seven years to perfect a thing. Some things I have been working on for twenty-five years—and some of them are still unsolved. My average would be about seven years. The incandescent light was the hardest one of all; it took many years not only of concentrated thought but also of world-wide research. The storage battery took eight years. It took even longer to perfect the phonograph.

Which do I consider my greatest invention? Well, my reply to that would be that I like the phonograph best. Doubtless this is because I love music. And then it has brought so much joy into millions of homes all over this country, and, indeed, all over the world. Music is so helpful to the human mind that it is naturally a source of satisfaction to me that I have helped in some way to make the very finest music available to millions who could not afford to pay the price and take the time necessary to hear the greatest artists sing and play.

Many inventions are not suitable for the people at large because of their carelessness. Before a thing can be marketed to the masses, it must be made practically fool-proof. Its operation must be made extremely simple. That is one reason, I think, why the phonograph has been so universally adopted. Even a child can operate it.

Another reason, is that people are far more willing to pay for being amused than for anything else.

One great trouble with the world to-day is that people wander from place to place, and are never satisfied with anything. They are shiftless and thoughtless. They revolt at buckling down and doing hard work and hard thinking. They refuse to take the time and the trouble to lay solid foundations. They are too superficial, too flighty, too easily bored. They fail to adopt the right spirit toward their life work, and consequently fail to enjoy the satisfaction and the happiness which comes from doing a job, no matter what it is, absolutely in the best way within their power. Failing to find the joy which they should find in accomplishing something, they turn to every imaginable variety of amusement. Instead of learning to drink in joy through their minds, they try to find it, without effort through their eyes and their ears—and sometimes their stomachs.

It is all because they won't think, won't think!

I-1921

XXX · MACHINE AND PROGRESS

It has been charged abroad and occasionally at home that we of the United States have become a machine-ridden people, that we are developing upon lines too completely mechanical. The very reverse is the truth. We are not mechanical enough. The machine has been the human being's most effective means of escape from bondage. Too many people, even now, remain bond-slaves to laborious hand-processes. Not through fewer, but through more machines, not through simpler, but through more complex machines, will men find avenues that lead into lives of greater opportunity and happiness.

We must substitute motors for muscles in a thousand new ways. A human brain is greatly hampered in its usefulness if it has only two hands of a man to do its bidding. There are machines each of which can do the work of a multitude of hands, when directed by one brain. That is efficiency.

Anything which tends to slow work down is waste. Every effort should be made to speed work up. Increased production means enlarged lives for mankind. Human hands alone can do no more than they did long ago by way of fast production. Only machines, not nerves and muscles, can increase men's output. We have scarcely seen the start of the mechanical age, and after it is under way we shall discover that it is also a mental age as never has been known before. One of the reasons it will be notably mental will be that it will be notably mechanical. It requires a surprising amount of complexity to displace the mechanical effort of the man. The difference between the automatic and the semi-automatic machine is very great. Its significance in industry is immense. But once the fully automatic has been achieved, the output and quality of the product will be greatly increased. All fully automatics, on account of their very complexity, require attendants of mental capacity greatly increased over that of men who are merely parts of semi-automatics.

There could be no greater waste than keeping good brains at work directing the hands of the bodies they control in the hand-execution of mechanical tasks because of the mere failure to invent and develop machines to execute those tasks better and faster than hand work can execute them under good brain direction. Man will progress in intellectual things according to his release from the mere motor-tasks.

The history of slavery is full of illustrations of the value of machinery. Slavery, the use of men as beasts of burden and as motors, was mental bondage for the men who thought they benefited by it, as well as physical bondage for the men they held in thrall. While slave labor was available, the brains of men in general were not stimulated to the creation of machinery. This was more disastrous in its general effects than was realized by the majority, even of those opposed to slavery. It meant that human beings all along the line, not only the enslaved but the enslavers, could not be released by machinery for efforts better and more elevating than those to which they had been habituated in the past. Progress of mind became impossible.

That is the reason why I call machinery the greatest of emancipators. I will go farther and say that human slavery will not have been fully abolished until every task now accomplished by human hands is turned out by some machine, if it can be done as well or better by a machine. Why chain a man, thus wasting him, to laborious work which a machine could do? All men cannot walk out of the shadow into the light until all men understand the foolishness of such procedure.

The shoe factory of to-day requires better employees than were required by the old processes of laborious, slow, hand work. Some of the old time cobblers were fine fellows who could think, but they would have thought far more and better if their ignorance of machinery had not shackled them to the awl and hand-hammer-driven peg, to the bristle-tipped waxed-end. These things did nothing then which now are not far better done by our machines. I have said that men's brains are bettered by machinery, if it is of the right sort. That with which we now make boots and shoes develops brains far more fully than work with the old tools did or could. This is proved by the fact that when, by working at machines, men's brains are improved sufficiently, the men who have shown ability to run the first machines are promoted to the operation of those which are now more complicated and run still faster, requiring of their operators' increased alertness and mentality.

There is no common-sense in the cry that machine work is monotonous. On the other hand it creates a good product, uniform and universally dependable, which is something hand-work never could do. Machine work robs the product of the ill-effects of man's changing physical and mental conditions. The hand worker's product is uneven. Far too much of it is too bad to enable it to compete successfully with the output of the machine.

Americans use more machinery than anybody else. I am told that American workers each can run six looms of a certain kind, Germans five, Frenchmen five, Englishmen (whose workers never have ceased agitating against machinery) five,—and Chinese one, the quality being the same when the cloth is inspected. If the Chinese should begin suddenly to use machinery extensively, it would be only a matter of time when they could run more machines than they can now. Their indicator numeral would go up in the scale. But at the start, one Chinese could run but one machine. The workers of the so-called "machinized" nations can operate the larger numbers I have stated because working with machines has much increased their mental development.

If we continue to increase machine production and the number of machines engaged at it, the next generation will be far beyond where we are now in its intelligence as well as in the possession of facilities for getting the good things out of life.

One of the most foolish things men say, and one which they often repeat, is that too much substitution of machine-work for hand-work will bring over-production. The idea is complete nonsense. There cannot be over-production of anything which men and women want, and their wants are unlimited except in so far as they are limited by the size of their stomachs. The stomach is the only part of man which can be fully satisfied. The yearning of man's brain for new knowledge and experience and for pleasanter and more comfortable surroundings never can be completely met. It is an appetite which cannot be appeased. Talk of over-production is a bugaboo.

A general benefit ensues inevitably from the increasing use of machinery. Not only do the workers benefit through the development enforced on them by the machines, but, in exact proportion as the machines enable the manufacturers to turn out more and better work, the sale of their manufactures is permitted at a decreased price. If the manufacturer can sell at a decreased price then, automatically, it becomes possible for the man of average income to have more things than theretofore. That man of average income has gained tremendously through the creation of machines. There is no doubt in my mind that in quantity production, so called, lies the greatest hope which now exists to cheer the human race. Quantity production cannot possibly occur without machinery. Therefore no man should rail against machine-power. It is application of good fertilizer to industry.

We use every known device of science, and continually seek for new ones, in our efforts to enlarge the production of our grain fields, our fruit orchards, and our vegetable gardens. What is that but striving to stimulate our plants and trees to quantity production? Are not the productive powers of men as worthy of good fertilizer? Machinery is the influence which enables men to do what stimulated plant life does to increase this year's output as compared with last year's to make certain for next year of more than this year's yields. It is as worthy an ambition to make two pairs of shoes where one was made before, that is, with the same human effort, as it is to devise agricultural means of making two blades of grass grow this year where only one grew last.

When objection to machinery has occurred among the workers it has been as foolish as is the refusal of men to accept any other opportunity for progress. Time was when printers all over New York City, and, indeed, the nation, struck or threatened to strike against typesetting machines, fearing that if they should come into general use fewer printers would be hired and at lower wages. The machine won, of course. And there are far more printers working now than were working then, and wages are higher. The economic status of the printer has much improved. So has his intelligence. So has his self-respect. He does not have to do things with his brains and muscles which a machine without brains can do better and faster. The printers of to-day would strike if you should try to take machines away from them.

The history of the typesetting machine is like that of every other machine which has been introduced to perform work previously done by hand; laboriously, slowly, expensively, and less perfectly. The sewing-machine, for instance, has increased by fifty-fold the employment in the fields which it affects.

Wherever something has compelled us to put in machinery to do work theretofore done by men's hands and muscles while brains have remained comparatively idle, all of us, and especially the men directly involved, have gained. If labor everywhere would strike against the use of men as animals instead of protesting against their use as human beings, it would show superior wisdom. Such a strike would have an unprecedentedly good effect on human life, for in very many of our most important activities the possibilities of machine development as an accessory to human intelligence and productiveness are, even yet, not fully understood.

X-1926

XXXI · THEY DO WHAT THEY LIKE TO DO

PEOPLE WILL NOT only do what they like to do—they overdo it 100 per cent. Most people overeat 100 per cent, and oversleep 100 per cent, because they like it. That extra 100 per cent makes them unhealthy and inefficient. The person who sleeps eight or ten hours a night is never fully asleep and never fully awake—they have only different degrees of doze through the twenty-four hours. Most people seem to think they must eat until they are no longer hungry. Most of their energies are taken up in digesting what they eat. I see what people eat, and for myself half as much is enough.

For myself I never found need of more than four or five hours' sleep in the twenty-four. I never dream. It's real sleep. When by chance I have taken more I wake dull and indolent. We are always hearing people talk about "loss of sleep" as a calamity. They better call it loss of time, vitality and opportunities. Just to satisfy my curiosity I have gone through files of the British Medical Journal and could find not a single case reported of anybody being hurt by loss of sleep. Insomnia is different entirely—but some people think they have insomnia if they can sleep only ten hours every night.

Now, I'm not offering advice. That's no use. Nobody takes advice. As I say, people do what they like to do and overdo it 100 per cent, and the same rule applies to the giving of advice that nobody pays any attention to. The world is badly overstocked with unused advice.

II-8-1921

XXXII · THE INVENTOR'S LOT

THE INVENTOR tries to meet the demand of a crazy civilization. Society is never prepared to receive any invention. Every new thing is resisted, and it takes years for the inventor to get people to listen to him and years more before it can be introduced, and when it is introduced our beautiful laws and court procedure are used by predatory commercialism to ruin the inventor. They don't leave him even enough to start a new invention.

I-5-1914

XXXIII · THE DESIRE FOR CHANGE

PERPETUAL YOUTH and virtual immortality on this earth would seem to me to be most undesirable. When the time comes, normal human beings do not desire abnormal extension of the earthly life-period. No dreamer about immortality has crystallized his dreams into a desire for a perpetual extension of such lives as we live here. Enough's enough of any human life as human lives are now. Those normal men who have reached the extreme limit of the human life cycle invariably are indifferent to death. They do not desire extension of the present existence. The group of entities which make up such a normal man's intelligence seek release from, rather than prolongation of, existence in the conditions and environments of this cycle so that they may enter another, whatever it may be. All through life humanity yearns for change, for without change progress is impossible and I am convinced that at the end of that which we call life this subconscious desire for something new is very great, and in many instances influential, no matter how the concious mind, trained by instinct and long habit to cling to this existence, may struggle to combat it. New scenes, new occupations, new emotions, new successes, —these all normal human beings strive for during this life. When they have had all of these that they can get out of it they must turn for change to whatever may come beyond.

I-1927

XXXIV · AGE AND ACHIEVEMENT

THE MAN who has reached the age of thirty-six has just about achieved readiness to discard the illusions built on the false theories for which wrong instruction and youthful ignorance previously have made him an easy mark. He is just beginning to get down to business. If he is really worth while he has passed through a series of hard knocks by that time. The useful man never leads the easy, sheltered, knockless, unshocked life. At thirty-six he ought to be prepared to deal with realities and after about that period in his life, until he is sixty, he should be able to handle them with a steadily increasing efficiency. Subsequently, if he has not injured his body by excess indulgence in any of the narcotics (and by this term I mean, here, liquor, tobacco, tea, and coffee), and if he has not eaten to excess, he very likely may continue to be achievingly efficient up to his eightieth birthday and in exceptional cases until ninety.

Then the curve turns sharply down. The cycle is approaching the end. At about that age the entities which form that man will be preparing to discard their old abode, which is that man, and enter upon a new cycle. Then and not till then men should, must, and do begin to step aside. If all men did so at the age of thirty-five the world of times to come would be virtually without achievement and leadership.

I-1927

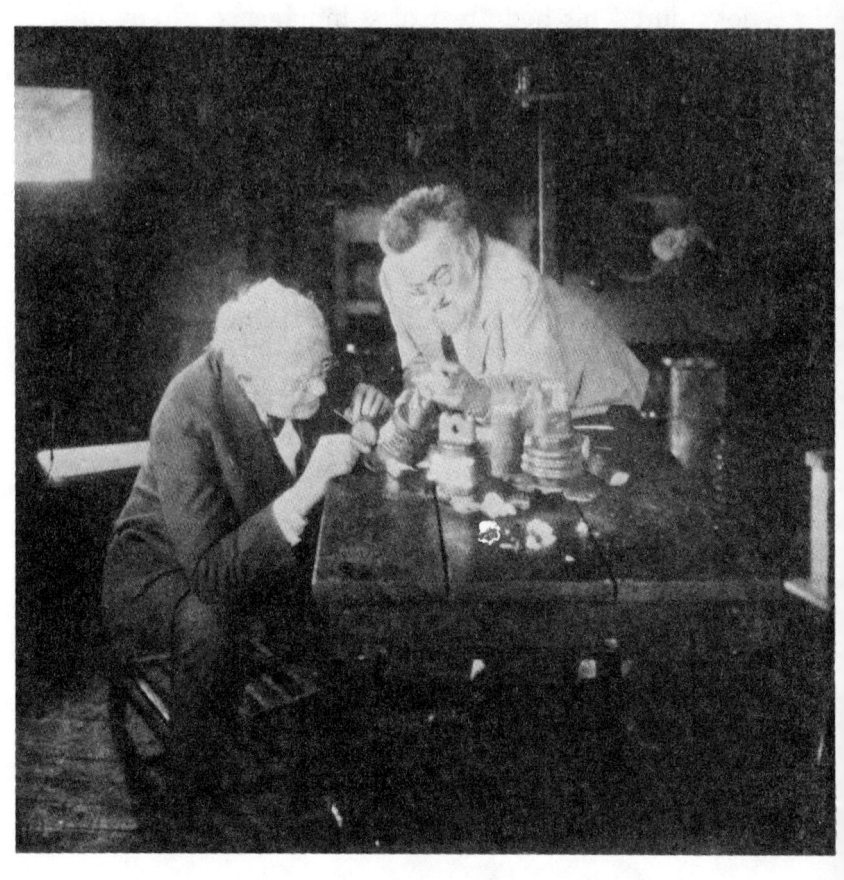

2. EDISON AND CHARLES P. STEINMETZ

VII
For a Better World

FOR A BETTER WORLD

XXXV · THE ECONOMICS OF FEAR

THERE IS NO DOUBT that economic conditions in our country are somewhat upset, but they are not so seriously disarranged that we cannot remedy them by grit, determination and hard work. Don't call it a panic. It is nothing but a period of depression, and nothing to worry over, provided we set ourselves resolutely to the task of overcoming it. These periods of depression come in recurring cycles. They are nothing new. The point to be driven home is that the country always recovers from them and goes forward with greater strides than ever before. We will get over this one, too. The tide already has begun to turn. Times are getting better now, slowly, of course, but surely. These periods of depression are caused by a faulty adjustment of our economic machine, or by it being thrown out of gear by some unusual force, such as war. The machine is all right; it will work properly as soon as the obstruction is removed.

The condition reminds me very much of a traffic block at one of the busy street crossings in New York, where vehicles sometimes become apparently inextricably locked. The expert traffic cop, however, by backing a car a little here, a truck there, by sending this team to the right and that one to the left, makes an opening through which the traffic begins to move smoothly, in fact, faster than before, for the drivers whip up a bit to make up for lost time.

The psychology of fear is the prime cause of the present depression. The people have been frightened out of good times, unnecessarily so, because our country and its economic conditions are fundamentally sound, and being sound they will finally triumph. "Truth crushed to earth will rise again." Of course we cannot expect the flush times, the big wages and big profits that we enjoyed during the war. The immense orders for war material, which gave such an impetus to both business and wages, ceased with the coming of peace. They both had to get back to normal, and during the period of readjustment some economic disturbances naturally arose.

Instead of bravely facing the changed conditions, timid souls, sensing in this disturbance a coming depression, began to pull in their money, and to hide it in their stocking. Merchants stopped buying, except in a hand-to-mouth way, fearing that the coming readjustments would reduce prices. The manufacturers and mine owners reduced their output, and curtailed the number of their employes. As the number of unemployed increased, it gave a text to the calamity howlers, who preached hard times from the housetops. The people became frightened, which resulted in further withdrawal of capital, which in turn brought a further discharge of help, and more calamity howling. It was a descending spiral, a senseless descent, because there was nothing materially the matter with the economic condition of our country, except that the people had become frightened at their own shadows.

Our job is to convert it into an ascending spiral, which can be accomplished if we can restore confidence, destroy the spectre of fear, and make the people believe in the soundness of our Government and our economic system. In order to do so, we must look conditions squarely in the face. We must each make personal sacrifices, and each of us put our shoulder to the wheel and push.

How shall we go about putting our unemployed to work? The first step is to prevail on these added workers in the industrial field to return to their prewar pursuits, and to help them get back. America, with her unlimited resources, her farms, mines and factories can afford work for all of her unemployed. The main thing is to bring the man and the job together, which can be done through employment bureaus. There are skeleton and inefficient bureaus throughout the country, but they should be energized and co-ordinated so as to work in perfect harmony with a national bureau, whose purpose and duty it should be to keep in touch with the labor needs of every section of the country, and broadcast this information, so that the local bureaus can send their surplus labor where it is needed. It may not be possible to secure the kind of work that a laborer wants, but it is possible to secure work for him. The bureaus should also advance him money for transportation to his new job.

America's fertile fields always welcome willing hands. Farm labor, while it may not be immensely profitable, is always self-supporting. It converts a man from a liability to an economic asset. The automobile has made farm life more pleasant; with the telegraph, telephone and automobile, it is possible for the farmer to keep in close touch with the city and outside world. The motor truck enables him to engage in more profitable farming. He can transport his produce to the city at much less cost, and from a much greater distance than was possible for him to do before its advent.

The next step toward relieving unemployment is the resumption of public work. This public work should be of a necessary character, "made jobs" are an economic loss. There is, however, plenty of necessary work to be done. Every city, State and the national Government must do a certain amount of public improvement, such as the building of schools, repairing of public buildings, making roads, laying sewers and improving public parks. This work should be done now. Some cities say that they have no money with which to carry on these improvements. They can issue bonds at a sufficient rate of interest to invite investment.

Now is not the time to cry poverty. Concerted effort on the part of the national, State and municipal governments can utilize a large number of our unemployed. In the meantime, it may be necessary to engage in some emergency relief work, but this is to be discouraged as far as possible. It is no cure for the depressed condition. It is like bailing out a leaking boat continuously, rather than taking the time to caulk it. A thousand dollars spent in giving men honest work will do more good than $10,000 used in pauperizing them. It is not charity, but an opportunity to make a living that our unemployed want.

Another obstruction in our economic machine is the uncertainty concerning future legislative enactments. The Congress should hasten to pass laws that will give assurance to capital and furnish it protection. Capital is timid at best. It hesitates to invest money in uncertainties, preferring to place it on an assured interest until it knows what expenses are to be attached in the form of tariffs, income and excess profit taxes, cost of labor and material. As soon as the Congress lets the capitalists know where they stand, how much it is going to cost to do business, what labor legislation is going to be passed, what is to be done about transportation and shipping and whether the freight rates are to be advanced or reduced, they can determine how far they can safely go in reopening their industries. The more favorable the legislation passed by the Congress is to business interests the more increase there will be in industry, and the larger the number of unemployed put to work. A dilatory and inefficient administration of national affairs does more to hinder the return of prosperity than any other agency.

We must increase our output. The most obvious way to do so is by exporting more of our produce. This cannot be done until the tariff question is definitely settled. Our trade with most foreign nations is at present largely a matter of barter, because their money is practically valueless—fiat money, with nothing to back it. You cannot back a steel engraving plant and a printing press. Americans are not willing to sell their supplies on any such security; as our dealings with them are necessarily a barter, before we can satisfactorily deal with them, we must know the definite tariff rates on which their produce will be admitted.

We must get back to normal living and spending, forget our fears, our extravagances and our niggardliness, and live as if it were ordinary times. During the war America lost its head. Money was so plentiful, such high prices could be obtained for commodities, jobs paying such big wages so easily could be secured, that we fairly wallowed in extravagance. Then came the reaction, and we went to the other extreme. At the first cry of hard times, and as a token of rebellion against high prices, we went on a 'buyer's strike.' I attended a dinner last Summer at which there were forty guests, all of them men of independent means. Noticing that the hats in the check room did not look particularly new, and having an inquisitive mind, I found out that twenty-nine of them were of last year's vintage. Naturally, the hat business has not been prosperous.

What we must do is to believe that normal times are close at hand and live accordingly. The manufacturer and miner, if he is optimistic, can, as far as the banks will carry him, make up stock for future delivery. The banker, if he is optimistic, can advance money to the manufacturer, as far as is consistent with business principles. The laborer must get back to normal by recognizing that war time wages are past, and accepting a reduction of wages that will enable his employer to sell his goods at a profit. The jobber and retailer must assist in the reorganization by charging off to profit and loss the difference between prices based on the present wage and the prices which he paid for his goods, and the consumer must begin buying normally. The whole people must work in unison with the definite aim of bringing back good times, which they can best do by living as if they were here already.

A restoration of confidence will do more to accomplish this end than any other factor. Let me emphasize that there is plenty of capital in the country to finance industry, provided it is safe to do so. That there are plenty of natural resources in our country to furnish the proper security to capital and to support many times the number of people that we now have. That there is nothing economically wrong with America. While other nations may be financially bankrupt, our money is worth one hundred cents on the dollar. That while our taxes are high they are not confiscatory, as practically they are in some other nations. That we have the best transport system in the world, with more miles of railroads, more automobiles, more and cheaper methods of getting our produce to market, and a normally free buying public to consume our produce.

There has been an indescribable something in the air that caused our fears, which in turn created the depressed economic condition. This something will disappear as a mist in the morning. As we gain confidence the bankers will lend more money, gradually, of course, but more. The mine operator will increase his output, the manufacturer will employ more workers. As the prices come down the people will go back to normal buying.

Good times are coming, and like the traffic block, everybody will whip up a bit to make up for lost time.
IX-29-1921

XXXVI · THE STANDARD OF GOLD

GOLD MAKES PRETTY jewelry and picture frames and is used effectively for filling teeth. Otherwise it is an almost wholly useless substance. Yet we hold it as the standard of all values.

The gold-standard system is largely fiction. Banks have a gold reserve of, say, fifty per cent of their note issue. This is fifty per cent alleged real reserve and fifty per cent pure gamble, the banks taking the gambling chance that the note holders will not call on them all at one time. Finally, if things go wrong, and the note holders begin to demand the fifty per cent gold, the banks fall back upon the credit of the Government and the merchants' notes through the Federal Reserve.

It seems absurd to me that all our values should be based on boxes of metal in any treasury. It is an absurdity, but everyone has been educated to believe that absurdity is common sense.

Before the invention of credit money, there was gold enough to function perfectly with the small amount of business that was transacted. Now it is otherwise. Just think of using gold as a standard of value in the highly organized financial and commercial system at present in vogue throughout the world! Under the present system our Government certifies to the amount of gold in disks and bars of metallic alloy. Then they are packed into boxes and kept traveling continuously all over the world—New York to London, London to Bombay, back to New York, and so on. The principal quantity we keep in vaults as an alleged support to our circulation medium. Other governments follow the same program.

I should think that values should be based not upon supplies of gold in treasury vaults—for gold is a commodity and must fluctuate—but upon the wholesale price of the necessaries of life; that is, production cost plus a reasonable profit at the point of production, as, for instance, the cost of coal at the mine or that of certain basic manufactured articles at the factory.

Why should not all the governments of the world come together and establish an international index of value for exchangeable necessaries of life in the countries producing them. Then the peoples of the different nations and the populations within each nation could do business by the infinitely simple system of plain barter. You have so much oil; well, I have so much wool or woolen goods. I want your oil. You want my wool or cloth. We might be governments or individuals; it would not matter.

A great amount of research and other work would need to be done before this system could be established, because of the different tastes and needs of the people. But what is better money than that based on certified commodities in government warehouses and merchants' short notes for goods actually sold and discounted by a bank taking currency issued by the Federal Reserve Bank, with notes as security?

We need not worry very much about a standard for

super-luxuries, but the prices of absolute necessities ought to be fixed. As it is, no man can tell how much food, clothing, pleasure, education, his labor will secure.

I-1922

XXXVII · NATIONS AND THE GOLD STANDARD

IF AN EFFORT had been made to bind the nations of the world for a period of fifty years it probably would have failed; if it had not failed but had gone through it never really could have been effective.

In the end a long-term agreement of that sort would have bred more trouble than it had been designed to prevent.

It is my belief that an agreement which goes on one year easily may be made the basis of others, which in a common sense succession may go on with occasional revision to meet changed conditions, giving perfect satisfaction, practically forever.

Such an agreement will establish the habit of agreement upon fundamentals; the habit of the past has been disagreement upon fundamentals.

Now, I think, the thing to do is to call a conference to take up the subject of the world's money-mechanism.

The problem is a gigantic complex, but it can be threshed out by experts even though we may feel sure that in it they will find tremendous difficulties.

Nations must do business with each other.

They cannot unless they know just what each other's money is, how much it actually is worth and whether it is going to be worth the same tomorrow and next week that it is worth today.

I have seen such a necessity for prompt action in this matter that I think the new conference should be convened as soon as possible.

As a financial investment nothing could be more promising to everyone who would be concerned.

The total cost of such a conference would not be greater than the loss which must accrue each day until it shall be held. Five minutes' loss during any financial day of the current week, due to the fact that things are as they are and not as they might be, indeed, probably would pay all of it.

The expenditure of money upon such a conference would be better than appropriations for relief. Analysis of the situation in Europe indicates that people over there are starving principally because their money is without a stable value. Stabilize it and there will be fewer calls for great relief funds.

Europe has no standard of value. We, in the United States, have destroyed for Europe the gold standard because we have accumulated in our financial centers the major portion of the whole world's gold supply.

We have not brought this about by greed, or, indeed, intention of any kind. The gold has come to us automatically in the way of business.

But it is here, the other nations are without it and something must be done.

Some of this gold must go back to the lands from which it came, to bolster up their currencies, to give them a standard of value and to put a partial guarantee behind their moneys.

It is curious, this matter of the gold standard.

Gold, really, is not valuable. In actuality something like two dollars an ounce ought to express its worth.

It has been given an utterly false value because it has been used as the money standard.

To my mind such an economic council of the nations would be quite as important as the conference for the limitation of armament.

Unless we get these money matters straightened out we may find ourselves in peace-time troubles quite as serious as those of war.

This conference, like that dealing with the limitation of armament, should be held at Washington, I think, for in the United States is held, at present, that vast mass of the world's gold which in some way must be distributed so as to bolster up the foreign money systems.

This is the most important of the several economic problems which are tying up the business of the world.

If the gold standard is to be maintained this gold must be distributed, else European nations cannot get back to smooth operation of their monetary systems.

That the problem can be solved and without much difficulty I have no doubt whatever. But the world's mind will have to find the method. I have not at hand enough data to permit me even to express a definite opinion as to what decisions should be reached. The thing is too complex for the formulation of a simple solvent.

That is why it demands a conference of the world's best minds.

But it is not beyond the genius of the world.

As a matter of fact I can see no reason why the experts of the great commercial banks in the world's financial centers should be unable to devise a plan whereby all currencies forthwith may be stabilized to a reasonable extent.

The point is that money, to be ready money, must have something behind it, and now much of that which is called money by the world has no tangible value at the back of it. It consists of promises to pay issued without guarantee.

Really there is in every country plenty of property which might be used as security to guarantee that country's money. The arrangement of the matter merely requires a plan and general agreement to it.

We must learn the new lessons as we learned the old ones. We must devise some system which will not break down.

There must be more co-operation among nations in these matters, and co-operation between nations cannot be arranged without consultation between nations.

The people blame the banks for everything—which is a sign that the people are not educated.

I wish we might excite the total population of this country with regard to this whole money question. Apparently we will not study subjects unless we are excited over them. The campaigns which defeated William Jennings Bryan saved the nation many millions and perhaps more than one immense disaster because they educated people in some phases of the economic problem.

With such a conference backed by, studied by and carefully reported by the newspapers we should find ourselves immensely benefited.

It would help our own financial system and perhaps would save that of Europe.

The burden of world leadership in such things rests on us and England. The hands of all the other nations at this moment are in the air in virtual surrender to despair.

The British are extremely sane, saner, possibly, than we are.

They are less sentimental and they have the best financial brains, I think, in the whole world. By 'best financial brains' I do not mean those which are merely cunning, smart, but those which actually are able. In this quality British financiers are superior to ours.

We have some fine men in our big commercial

banks, but unfortunately they are handicapped by the fact that almost all of them are under that unwarranted suspicion of the banker which has become a habit with us. Our thinkers do not seem able to separate the big commercial banks from the speculative interests. Really they are as different as black from white.

But we do not lack ability.

A good many men fit to represent us, protect us, and help the world at such a conference could be found among the very institutions which now are generally and mistakenly under such suspicion. They are of high character and fine mental type. They have studied economics and have had experience.

They are the resultant of natural selection. It is pretty hard for any man to get to be the head of a great commercial bank unless he has the stuff in him. Bluff won't last long in a job like that.

With such men from our own country and with the best from all the others sitting at a table, with many points of view all honestly endeavoring to understand and trying to report and elucidate for their readers fairly and fully, much would be accomplished.

Economic education is what such people need and they cannot get it without the great public discussion which would come out of an economic conference.

We must keep on experimenting in warfare at the same time, endeavoring to learn how to produce the most deadly materials and weapons so that if we slip because someone declares a treaty to be a scrap of paper we shall have men educated in the processes of the things which we must do, and able, with our immense mechanical resources at their disposition, to do them very quickly.

But never for a single moment must we forget the economic problem.

Such study as I have suggested of war methods would be preparation in a new and reasonable sense.

I would not burden the great body of our citizenship with heavy taxes.

Suppose we have only one piece of artillery, developed after elaborate experiment and known to be absolutely perfect—the super-gun of all artillery, with every process for its manufacture carefully worked out. If war should come, even unexpectedly, we very quickly could proceed to quantity production from that model. We could be ready to fight soon enough.

I believe in just that sort of thing.

We need disarmament, but, at the same time, we need capacity for armament. I believe all nations should have that.

Teach the world that whoever starts a row very quickly will be subject to attack by terrible, death-dealing gases, by incredible swarms of aircraft, highly efficient and quickly manufactured, and the row will not be started.

In the meantime the whole world will not be groaning under the expense of keeping up continually a vast armament which, after all, must be principally notable through the fact that it becomes so quickly obsolete.

These things are important, but even more important is such economic knowledge as will enable us to readjust and actually get back to normal after any period of abnormality.

We cannot get on our feet until we have a market for our goods, and, curiously enough, the world cannot get on its feet until we stand firmly upon ours.

We cannot have a market for our goods till the European monies have been stabilized.

To restore exchange to normal would be a great thing for us. It would help us as much as it would help the British.

It sometimes is bad business to keep bankrupts in their bankruptcy. Every day wise creditors in ordinary business lend new sums to their bankrupt debtors in order that they may start again. Business recognizes this as a good policy as long as the debtor's character, experience and record are good.

We should reason thus when we think of England and France. It is infinitely important to us that they should be back upon their feet.

I-1-1922

VIII
The Realms Beyond

THE REALMS BEYOND

XXXVIII · LIFE AFTER DEATH

THE THING which first struck me was the absurdity of expecting "spirits" to waste their time operating such cumbrous, unscientific media as tables, chairs, and the ouija board with its letters. My convinced belief is merely that if ever the question of life after death, or pyschic phenomena generally, is to be solved, it will have to be put on a scientific basis, as chemistry is put, and withdrawn from the hands of the charlatan and the "medium."

My business has been, and is, to give the scientific investigator—or, for that matter, the unscientific—an apparatus which, like the compass of the seaman, will put their investigations upon a scientific basis. This apparatus may perhaps most readily be described as a sort of valve. In exactly the same way as a megaphone increases many times the volume and carrying power of the human voice, so with my "valve", whatever original force is used upon it is increased enormously for purposes of registration of the phenomena behind it. It is exactly on the lines of the tiny valve which in a modern power-house can be operated by the finger of a man and so release a hundred thousand horse-power.

Now, I don't make any claims whatever to prove that the human personality survives what we call "death." All I claim is that any effort caught by my apparatus will be magnified many times, and it does not matter how slight is the effort, it will be sufficient to record whatever there is to be recorded.

Frankly, I do not accept the present theories about life and death. I believe, rightly or wrongly, that life is undestructible, it is true, and I also believe that there has always been a fixed quantity of life on this planet, and that this quantity can neither be increased nor decreased. But that does not mean that I believe the survival of personality has been proved—as yet. Perhaps it may be one day. Perhaps some apparatus upon the lines of my "valve" may prove it, but that day is not yet, nor have I as yet secured any results to definitely prove such survival.

What I believe is that our bodies are made up of myriads of units of life. Our body is not itself *the* unit of life or *a* unit of life. It is the tiny entities which may be the cells that are the units of life.

Everything that pertains to life is still living, and cannot be destroyed. Everything that pertains to life is still subject to the laws of animal life. We have myriads of cells, and it is the inhabitants in these cells, inhabitants which themselves are beyond the limits of the microscope, which vitalize and "run" our body.

To put it in another way, I believe that these life-units of which I have spoken band themselves together in countless millions and billions in order to make a man. We have too facilely assumed that each one of us is himself a unit, just as we have assumed that the horse or dog is each a unit of life. This, I am convinced, is wrong thinking. The fact is that these "life-units" are too tiny to be seen even by the most high-powered microscope, and so we have assumed that the unit is the man which we can see, and have ignored the existence of the real life-units, which are those we cannot see.

There is nothing to prevent these entities from carrying on the varied work of the human body. I have had the calculations made, and the theory of the electron is, in my view, satisfactory, and makes it quite possible to have a highly organized and developed entity like the human body made up of myriads of electrons, themselves invisible.

Further, I believe that these life-units themselves possess memory. If a man burns his hand, the skin will grow in exactly the same pattern again, and with the same lines as the hand originally had before the accident. Now, it would be quite impossible for those hundreds of fine lines to be meticulously reproduced if there were no memory for detail behind the rebuilding of them. The skin does not grow that way and in exactly the same pattern again "by chance." There is no chance.

But are all these life-units, or entities, possessed of the same memory, or are some, so to speak, the builders' labourers, and are others the units which direct those labourers?

It may be that the great mass of them are workers and a tiny minority directors of the work. That is not a matter about which we can speak with any certainty.

But what one can say with some assurance is that these entities cannot be destroyed, and that there is a fixed number of them. They may assemble and reassemble in a thousand different forms from a starfish to a man, but they are the same entities.

No man today can set the line as to where "life" begins and ends. Even in the formation of crystals we see a definite ordered plan at work. Certain solutions will always form a particular kind of crystal, without variation. It is not impossible that these life-entities are at work in the mineral and plant, as in what we call the "animal" world.

In connection with the problem of life after death, the thing that matters is what happens to what one may call the "master" entities—those that direct the others. Eighty-two remarkable operations on the brain have definitely proved that the seat of our personality lies in that part of the brain known as the fold of Broca. It is not unreasonable to suppose that these entities which direct reside within this fold. The supreme problem is what becomes of these master entities after what we call death, when they leave the body.

The point is whether these directing entities remain together after the death of the body in which they have been residing, or whether they go about the universe after breaking up. If they break up and no longer remain as an ensemble, then it looks to me that our personality does not survive death; that is, we do not survive death as individuals.

If they do break up and do not remain together after the death of the body, then that would mean that the eternal life which so many of us earnestly desire would not be the eternal life and persistence of the individual, as individual, but would be an impersonal eternal life—for, whatever happens to the life-units, or whatever forms they may assume, it is at least assured that they themselves live forever.

I do hope myself that personality survives and that we persist. If we do persist upon the other side of the grave, then my apparatus, with its extraordinary delicacy, should one day give us the proof of that persistence, and so of our own eternal life.

VIII-1922

XXXIX · LIFE'S FLASHBACKS

WE DO NOT REMEMBER. A certain group of our little people do this for us. They live in that part of the brain which has become known as the "fold of Broca."

Broca discovered and proved that everything we call memory goes on in a little strip not much more than a quarter of an inch long. That is where the little people live who keep our records for us.

Some of the little peoples who enable us to remember things do nothing else during our entire lives but watch moving picture shows. Everything that comes in through the eyes comes in the form of moving pictures. These pictures come so rapidly that, like the pictures on a screen, they seem to be but one picture, but in fact they are millions. The optic nerves bring the pictures through the small holes in the front of our skulls into our brains where the little peoples whose function it is to remember can see them. We do not remember everything we see because everything is not worth remembering. Little Peoples, like "big peoples," are of various degrees of intelligence. Some will choose to remember what others will choose to forget. But whatever their intelligence, they all seem to be impressed by the startling and the unusual. The thing is remembered that makes an impression. When a human being is young and his little memory-people have empty record cases, many things make an impression. That is why so many childhood memories linger throughout our lives.

A man was here the other day who had recently visited the school-house he attended when he was five years old. He told me that as he approached the place everything seemed much as he had left it almost half a century before: the hill down which he used to coast had somewhat flattened out; it was not the little Matterhorn, the memory of which he had carried with him so many years, but a very gentle slope. As he drew nearer the little building his mind was flooded with memories; this thing, that thing, and the other thing—there they were just as he had left them. But when he approached one of the side windows and looked into the room where he learned the alphabet, he got a great shock. Something was wrong with the windows! They were too low. As he looked through the little panes of glass he became distinctly uncomfortable. What was the matter? Then the answer came to him. The last time he had looked through that window he was so short that he had to grab hold of the sill to pull himself up. He had grown so tall that his eyes were perhaps three feet above the sill.

Now see what had happened. For more than forty years some of the little people in this man's brain had carried about with them a certain recollection about those window sills. The recollection was that the sills were so high one could not look through the windows without pulling himself up. Waking or sleeping, wherever he went during those forty-odd years, that recollection was with the man, though he did not know it. During this time, the substance of his body, including his brain, had changed several times, but the little peoples that live in the cells had not changed. The moment the little peoples in that man's optic nerves began to see moving pictures of those old window sills and sent the message back to the brain, some of the little people in the fold of Broca began to stir. They had heard about those window sills before. They were so high that nobody could look through them without pulling himself up!

There may be twelve or fifteen shifts that change about and are on duty at different times like men in a factory. I infer this from the fact that we sometimes have to send for the particular ones that have the records we want. That is what we do, I think, when we cudgel our memories for the things we want to recall. We have forgotten a man's name, for instance. We ask the shift of little peoples who happen to be on duty, "What is that man's name?" They were not on duty when the name was given to them to remember and they don't know. After a while, suggestion or something else summons the shift that has the name and they give it. I therefore take it that the possession of what is called a good memory really means the possession of the ability to summon the particular groups of little peoples who have the records we want. Haven't you noticed that when you get in touch with the right group the thing you want to recall comes crashing into your consciousness with no evidence whatever of impaired vitality? The little peoples, who have remembered perfectly, seem almost to shout at you the information you want. Therefore it seems likely that remembering a thing is all a matter of getting in touch with the shift that was on duty when the recording was done.

These little intelligences inhabit human bodies just to get experience. They seem to crave it. As I see it, something like this happens: Billions of little peoples, perhaps, come together in a certain individual. Some want to do one thing and some another. Some have high ideals and some have not. For a while, they fight out their differences and then the stronger group takes charge and this group dominates the man's life. If the minority is willing to be disciplined and to conform there is harmony or at any rate something that approximates it. But oftentimes the minority is not willing to conform. It is outraged at what it conceives to be the indignities that the majority heaps upon it. Minorities then sometimes say, "To hell with this place; let's get out of it." They refuse to do their appointed work in the man's body, he sickens and dies, and the minority gets out, as does too, of course, the majority. They are all set free to seek new experience somewhere else.

I should like to think that the recollections of experiences in one human life are carried forward through an endless succession of other lives. If the same little peoples were forever grouped together we should then have immortality and, what is perhaps more important, we should be able to begin each new experience with all the wisdom that we had gained during the ones that preceded it. This, however, is not what happens. Each generation is not able to profit from the mistakes of its ancestors. Each generation commits most of the same follies that have been committed since the beginning of time.

Nevertheless, I believe that some of our experiences are carried forward into succeeding generations. How else shall we account for what we may call inherited wisdom? Put your finger in a sleeping baby's hand. What does the baby do? It closes its hand on your fingers. Why? Because some of the little peoples in this baby remember the time when their forefathers lived in trees and it was necessary, to keep from falling and breaking their necks, to close their hands upon the limbs of trees.

What we call "inborn traits" are recollections of earlier experiences that the little peoples have brought along with them. Take an Indian baby, for instance. No matter how hard or how long you may try, you can never make a white man out of that baby. The little peoples in the baby will not permit you to do so. They have their ideas, gained from preceding experiences, of what a human being should do. You may repress these little peoples to the point where you believe you have made an Indian into a white man, but, when you least expect it, they will jump out at you and startle you with a war whoop. Of course, what you do to the red little peoples will constitute part of the recollections that they will carry on into their next life-experience; and when there have been enough such experiences the Indian's "inborn traits" will have been changed.

That is about the way I look at it. I do not see how there could be any such thing as carrying from one person to another the bulk of the recollections that the little peoples have as they go along. These minute intelligences that carry our records would become so burdened, if they did not forget most of their experiences, that they would have no further capacity for memorizing. And inasmuch as the same little peoples never reassemble in another body, there can be no such thing as the perpetuation of the individual in another earth-life. Such things can happen, as they say, "only in the movies" or in literature. Rudyard Kipling, in one of his best stories, had a London bank clerk get a glimpse of a former incarnation when he was a Greek galley slave. That was literature, but it was not science.

III-21-1925

XXXX · MEMORY UNITS

IF MY THEORY IS CORRECT—that the machine called man is only a mass of dead matter and that the real life is in the millions of individual units which navigate this machine, and if on the destruction of the machine these individual units keep together, including those which have charge of memory (which is our personality)—then I think it is possible to devise apparatus to receive communications, if they desire to make them. It will be very difficult, as each individual unit, as to size, is beyond the limit of our present microscopes.

When I was a little boy, persistently trying to find out how the telegraph worked and why, the best explanation I ever got was from an old Scotch line repairer who said that if you had a dog like a dachshund long enough to reach from Edinburgh to London, if you pulled his tail in Edinburgh he would bark in London. I could understand that. But it was hard to get at what it was that went through the dog or over the wire.

II-8-1921

XXXXI • THE MYSTERY OF LIFE

I BELIEVE all the old and accepted theories of the origin of life to be fundamentally wrong.

Down in Florida, where I have a place, there is a bush which grows in the ocean—that is, it seems to be a bush. Really it is animal matter built into bush form by the efforts of thousands of insects; it is the work of highly organized individuals massed in a crowd for the purpose of the building. The uninformed who see it, native whites and negroes, believe this insect-aggregate to be a vegetable individual—a sea-tree.

Almost all men, even those whom we accept as best informed, make a similar mistake with regard to that which we denominate as a man, or a cat, or an elephant. We think the man a unit, that he is just a man; we think the cat a unit, that it is just a cat; we think the elephant a unit, that it is just an elephant.

I am convinced that such thinking is basically in error. Like the "bush" in the sea near my Florida home, the man, the cat, the elephant are collections of units. The insect-built "bush" seems to be a unit, an individual. The man does. The cat does. The elephant does. But it is only seeming.

Each is made up of many individuals gathered in a community, and it is the community. The unit which makes it up may be too small even for the microscope to see. Everything which we can see is a manifestation of community, not of individual effort.

The mystery of life would be inexplicable were it not for this. We say a man dies. Perhaps, in a sense, the term is accurate when the aggregate which we have called a man ceases to function as an aggregate and therefore no longer can be called a man; but the expression is not at all accurate if by it we mean that the life which kept that man at work or at play ceases to exist. Life does not cease to exist.

The life-units which have formed that man do not die. They merely pass out of the unimportant mechanism which they have been inhabiting, which has been called a man and has been mistaken for an individual, and select some other habitat or habitats. Perhaps they become the animating force of something else or many other things.

The theory which generally maintains about the origin of life seems to me to be unreasonable. We can't get something out of nothing. Life can't make life. Life is. It is not made.

Another thing which continually puzzled me, for a long time, was that nature seemed to be so horribly cruel. I could not acount for it. Finally, I have come to the conclusion that it is not true.

It is only apparent. Really those things which seem to be manifestations of nature's cruelty are merely episodes of competition between groups which covet one another's machines, one feeling that the possession of another's might help it better to meet the exigencies of the environment with which it finds itself surrounded. Take the supposed cruelty of the shark toward the cod for example; it probably is the effort of the vast swarm of individuals which make up the shark to obtain for its own purposes the mechanism of the group which inhabits the cod, has built the cod, and has given it the appearance and the functions of what we call "individual life." Real life is not lost at all in such a struggle. Thus, I believe that really it is not cruelty at all when the battle brings a complete and not merely a partial victory, when the victim is "killed," as we erroneously say and think, and not wounded and left "living" and in pain.

That is the only theory which seems reasonable to me with regard to that which we have denominated the "life-and-death struggle."

Then, if the individual is not the unit, what is? Obviously, the unit must be the smallest complete entity among those which make up the aggregate which we erroneously have called the individual. Very well. Then how small can a unit be and how complicated?

That must depend upon the fineness of matter. Smallness of units must accord with the ultimate fineness of matter. And life is individual to the unit and not to the aggregate of units. It is probable that the units are so small that, as yet, no microscope powerful enough to distinguish them as individuals has been created.

If we accept this as fact, another question arises: Is matter fine enough to permit units of such minute size to be very complicated?

We need not worry about that. The electron theory gives to it a reply which is wholly satisfactory. I have had the matter roughly calculated mathematically and have at hand the data of the calculation. I am sure that a highly organized entity, consisting of millions of electrons, still remaining too small to be visible through any existing microscope, is possible.

Ink your finger, as the police might that of a criminal, and then press it upon paper, thus recording the many tiny whorls which indent its skin. Then seriously burn it, so as to take the skin all off, and when it heals—that is, when the skin forms anew—ink it again and again press it upon paper. It will record whorls precisely similar to those which you had burned away. Who built the new in duplicate of the old? Nature?

No. Nature would not take the trouble to remember such unimportant details. The new were built by the units of the swarm, and the exactness with which the old were reproduced is due to the fact that the swarm has memory.

If a bridge falls, we rebuild it. If there should come along an outsider, say, a man from Mars with eyes so coarse in their functioning (a reasonable thought) that he could not see anything so small as a human workman, but acute enough so that he could see the the ruins of the old bridge and the new structure erected to take its place, he would say that the old bridge had died and nature had grown a new one. Again, if this creature, unable to see anything as small as a man, but able to see big things, like our larger ships and say, sky-scrapers, were to examine our world, he would think the ships and sky-scrapers were natural growths. He never would dream that man had built them, for he never would be able to see man. The fact that we attribute to nature so many creative achievements is proof of our ignorance and the inadequacy of our power of observation.

The individuals in the aggregate which we call a "man," the members of the swarm which (to some extent by chance) have collected to make that man, are ninety-five per cent workers and five per cent directors. The workers cannot loaf or stop, even though something may compel them from their habitat, that which has been the "body" of a "man." They must go to something else to build, as, for instance, to corn, a tree, grass—whatever may be—always working under the direction of the higher type among them. These, by the way, will be responsible, as they dominate or fail to, or in accordance with their aspirations, for the character of that which now is built.

In the case of a "man," for example, he may be "bad" or "good," in accordance with the trend of these dominant individuals or in accordance with the majority quality of the individuals which have gathered, more or less by chance, in the swarm which makes him up. He is "good" if "good" individuals are more numerous in it and dominate, and "bad" if the reverse occurs. The theory explains many things. Among these is the hitherto mysterious force called the "subconscious mind."

Instances of startling ability, such as that, for example, which characterizes a Rockefeller, are beginning to indicate to me the chance gathering into swarms of individuals in which qualities of a certain kind are paramount.

In the institute which bears the Rockefeller name, and which, by the way, was endowed with some of the millions which the collective genius of the assembled Rockefeller intelligence has gathered, parts of a chicken "killed" years ago—that is to say, then dismembered so completely that, were the old beliefs accurate, the process must have caused death and must have been followed by decay unless some method of artificial preservation had been resorted to—still "live" and "grow" in gelatine-filled glass jars provided for the purpose of the experiment. The cells—that is, the communes or groups of individuals which originally built that chicken—still are sending out workers, and these continue building. This is because the environment surrounding them is kept constantly favorable to their work despite the "death" of the "individual"—the aggregate called a "chicken."

Now, let us think about that chicken's origin. The accepted age-old theory is that it was the development of an egg to which the life of the mother hen had imparted part of itself, and that this developed until, within the egg, an embryonic chick was formed, which, growing, became perfect and strong, broke the shell, and appeared, a fully developed baby fowl. As a matter of fact, if the theory upon which I work is accurate, the egg from which the chicken came held the nucleus indeed, but held nothing which could be responsible for all that afterward brought about the formation of the chicken. That, I am beginning to believe, entered this egg from the outside.

It is generally contended that all which is necessary in order that a chicken may be built is fertilized egg, and that, under favorable conditions, this egg develops into the chicken through the working of forces within itself. I do not believe this. I believe that what I have called a "swarm," liberated from something else, finds this nucleus from the outside, and, accepting it as its new home, goes into it and starts to build this or that kind of chicken according to the indication of the nucleus.

Then comes the inevitable question: "Can life come out of life in unlimited reproduction?" Already I have expressed a negative opinion, with regard to this by saying: "Life can't make life. Life is." I do not believe the affirmative reply, which so generally is accepted. Had that affirmative theory been accurate, the earth long since would have been covered and smothered with all kinds of life. It is obvious that there must be some limit to reproduction. "Bad years" and "good years" for corn, for instance, could not explain the situation as it really is.

We don't know what the units of life are or what the requisites of their existence. It may be that they can live and prowl about in the ether of space and do not in the least require our atmosphere or soil. If so, earth-life can have accessions from the mysterious realms beyond our atmosphere. Probably that is how we got here in the first place, how life got here. The thought that life originated on this insignificantly little and comparatively unimportant sphere to me seems inconceivably egotistical.

As a matter of fact, the manner of the genesis of life upon this earth, I think, was this: After the earth cooled of the great heat of its assemblage, life-units came to it through space, into which they had been thrown from some other more developed sphere or spheres. Reaching the earth, they adapted themselves to the environment they found here; and then began the evolution of the various species as we have them, each "growing" individual being a collection of cell-communes.

I think this theory will explain special abilities better than any other. It will rid the world of harmful superstitions such as those of spiritualism. It will bring order out of the chaos of much of that puzzlement which we endeavor to accept as reasoning with regard to the creation and the genesis of man.

I have spoken about extraordinary developments of so-called genius in individuals. Special ability must result if, by some fortuitous chance, a collection, or swarm (I find myself accepting that word as descriptive) chances to be made up of entities of very high class along one particular line. Affinity, the attraction of like for like, probably plays its part in the formation of such collections. There have been hundreds of cases of extraordinary significance.

Another question which must be answered before I can proceed on the intelligent development of this theory is: "Could such a little thing as I have in mind travel through the ether of space or only through the air?" If it could travel through the air only, then its progress would be slow. If it could travel through the ether, it could proceed at the rate of a hundred and eighty thousand miles a second, going a distance equivalent to the circumference of the earth in one-four-hundred-and-twentieth of a minute. There, as elsewhere in the general problem, is work for a mathematician who is very expert.

There is work here, also, for an expert botanist, because the line between animal and vegetable life is so very narrow. And there remains for determination the line between "live" and "dead" matter and between movable and fixed life.

In the early moments of this paper, I spoke about what seems to be but is not a "sea-bush" that grows in the water near my winter place in Florida. A certain class of organized, living beings, large enough even to be seen with the naked eye, builds structures which appear to be but are not plants, being nothing more nor less than swarms of insects gathered in that form in order that they may get food conveniently. Consider the sponge. It seems vegetable, but is animal. Investigate further, and you will find it to be an aggregate which has been built by a group of insects.

It is impossible to accept as fact all the apparent testimony of appearances. In geological ages, all of a certain type of crustacean creatures suddenly disappeared, and quite a different type came into being. The swarms that had built the first had not been annihilated, but the environment had changed, and, in order to meet its new conditions, they built mechanisms of another pattern. One mechanism has been replaced by another of a different type many times in the world's history. Changed conditions not only require but force new forms. When a new environment replaces an old one, old forces build in new ways, in order to adapt themselves to altered circumstances.

Doubtless something of the sort will happen many times again. Certain animals that we know much about have been changed entirely in order to meet altered environment, and of this we have incontrovertible evidence. For instance, the elephant used to be a woolly beast. He ceased to be. He didn't change himself. The animal doesn't know anything about such changes. It is the group which changes him, working quite beyond his consciousness. The individual members of the swarm—that is, its leaders—realize the new necessities and begin to meet them gradually and with invariable intelligence. They stop building the old forms; they stopped building wool on the outside of the elephant when the elephant's environment became tropical. When the swarm finds wool unnecessary, wool, then, is dispensed with.

Swarms do it all. The daisy has been the same for, say, fifty thousand years. Then comes a variation. Perhaps the daisy becomes blue. How could one daisy do that? Some disturbance of the swarm that built that daisy must be responsible for the change.

The absurdity of our present theories seems pitiful

to me. "Nature does it!" What of that remark? It really means nothing, takes us nowhere. Botanists and allied scientists may prove me to be all wrong in saying that. That will not worry me if they will produce something which really will be reasonable. It will take thought, deep thought, and that high mathematical skill which I have mentioned to discover how many individuals can live in each cell; for a cell cannot be the unit of organized matter; it must be a group of organisms—a fixed commune.

I want some one to start along a new line of thought with regard to these and kindred subjects. We have been accepting old-established theories with a complacency unworthy even of our present imperfect mental grasp. We need fresh brain-energy among our scientists, new bravery, new initiative. Einstein has shown the world the sort of thought it needs, and it needs it along many lines. The more Einsteins we can get, the better. I wish we had an Einstein in every branch of science.

Many great discoveries remain to be made. We must start anew in many things, rejecting the old theories as Einstein did, building along new lines as Einstein did, fearing nothing any more than Einstein did.

It is not impossible that, when we find the ultimate unit of life, we shall learn that the journey through far space never could harm it and that there is very little that could stop it. Remember that it is smaller, infinitely, than anything the microscope can see. I believe the ultimate life-particle could go through glass with the greatest ease, and that not the highest or the lowest temperature known to human science could harm it. Such units of life could have come, and possibly still are coming, without injury through the cold of space. We know of microbes which will endure through four degrees above absolute zero, and some are so small that they can be forced through porcelain.

We human beings are colloids, not crystals; and we are in the best possible general environment for colloids. We never use crystals in our body-building if we can avoid them.

It is quite conceivable that these entities with which life starts have intelligence sufficient for the initiation of new lines of endeavor from time to time, as occasion or necessity for new lines arises. There is that hairless elephant; there is that blue daisy; there are countless changed and changing forms. That is the De Vries theory, which opposes the Darwinian theory of the origin of species.

The little entities are fine chemists. They can make an alkali so strong that it will displace from its salts the chemist's master alkali, potassium, and they must be close to ultimate matter, for they decompose salt into sodium and hydrochloric acid. Obviously, it will take great chemical as well as great mathematical knowledge to cope with the problems which they offer, but the world has, or will have, men who can do it. Even now there is the wonderful Japanese, Takamini, who discovered adrenalin, that extraordinary astringent which is manufactured by a gland and controls blood-pressure.

There is a significant instance, an illustration! It is the product of a gland, not an effort of intelligence, which controls blood-pressure. The brains of men have little to do with the control of the bodies of men. Tell me that our brains are the sole seat of our intelligence? Why, seven-tenths of the action of our bodies is quite automatic—that is, entirely beyond and dissociated from brain-control. The brain does not control the circulation of the blood, the action of the lungs, stomach, or bowels, growth of any of the vital processes. It is controlled by them. Nothing could be more absurd than to regard the brain as the exclusive seat of knowledge. Knowledge is everywhere throughout our being and throughout all other beings, inanimate, perhaps, as well as animate.

It is everywhere. In the animal, human or otherwise, the head is merely the chief office in which orders are originated and from which they are distributed. The five senses realize, understand, and meet the conditions which exist outside the body. The brain is occupied by the high-class workers. They have charge. The balance are, I might say, the proletariat. But it is dangerous (as many politicians have discovered) to assume that any proletariat is without intelligence. Those among this proletariat who show special ability may achieve promotion, moving upward to the higher tasks, I think, as men developing special talents in industry may move upward. Perhaps it is this process which slowly is making us more civilized.

Now, I shall express another thought which may seem startling. I believe these swarms, or, at least, the individuals which make up these swarms, live forever. Individuals among the entities which form them may change their habitat, leaving one swarm and joining another, so to speak, building corn, for instance, to-day and chickens to-morrow, in accordance with the material which they find at hand to work with. It is not impossible that the chief workers may keep together, from time to time changing their environment as circumstances may dictate, but I think evidence exists that the workers separate when a job on which they have been occupied is finished, and go to find new tasks with little or no regard for old companionships. This simply is a repetition, and perhaps the fundamental pattern of those processes which we find necessary in our ordinary lives. The personality-swarm abides within the fold of Broca, which, from eighty-two surgical operations, is known to be the seat of memory. If this swarm keeps together after body-death, our personality still lives.

It is the most complicated of subjects, opening up

very novel lines of reflection. That thought of the swarms is fascinating. A swarm, any swarm, easily might contain beings which knew how to build us as we were when we were chimpanzees or even as we were when we were fishes; I understand that in one period while we are in embryo we have the gills of fish, which slowly slough away before our actual birth.

I think it is certain that, if our environment in future changes as materially as it has in the past, alterations as great as that from fish to man and from gills to noses will occur in the course of future ages. Then what shall we be?

I have very vivid recollections of a motor journey through Switzerland not long before the World War began. As it progressed, I saw the effect of environment upon myself. If we went to a hotel in a small town far from steam- or water-power, and therefore without electric light, we found everyone in it going to bed at half-past eight or nine o'clock. In other towns, where there was electric light, product of developed water-power from the Alps, the people didn't go to bed till half-past eleven or midnight. They were alive and very likely out on the streets during those extra hours. We are virtually dead when we are asleep; that is, we then have no productive mental life, and no mental life which is not productive counts. Where there was light, we lived longer in the same length of time. Put a developed human being into an environment where there is no efficient artificial light and he must degenerate. Put an undeveloped human being into an environment where there is artificial light and he will improve.

Environment makes immense changes in animals, and it is interesting and hopeful to note that the environment of human beings is improving more rapily than that of other animals. Perhaps, for an ant or a gnat, it is not changing at all, although primary changes are progressing in the world itself. Earthquake shocks, like those which recently occurred in Mexico, prove that the world is shrinking. They are the convulsions attending permanent alterations in the earth's size and shape, and indicate the release of strains.

V-1920

XXXXII • SPIRITUALISM

A GREAT DEAL is being written and said about spiritualism these days, but the methods and apparatus used are just a lot of unscientific nonsense. I don't say that all these so-called mediums are simply fakers scheming to fool the public and line their own pockets. Some of them may be sincere enough. They may really have gotten themselves into such a state of mind, that they imagine they are in communication with spirits.

I have a theory of my own which would explain scientifically the existence in us of what is termed our "subconscious minds." It is quite possible that those spiritualists who declare they receive communications from another world allow their subconscious minds to predominate over their ordinary, everyday minds, and permit themselves to become, in a sense, hypnotized into thinking that their imaginings are actualities, that what they imagine as occurring, while they are in this mental state, really *has* occurred.

But that we receive communications from another realm of life, or that we have—as yet—any means, or method, through which we could establish this communication, is quite another thing. Certain of the methods now in use are so crude, so childish, so unscientific, that it is amazing how so many rational human beings can take any stock in them. If we ever do succeed in establishing communication with personalities which have left this present life, it certainly won't be through any of the childish contraptions which seem so silly to the scientist.

I have been at work for some time building an apparatus to see if it is possible for personalities which have left this earth to communicate with us. If this is ever accomplished, it will be accomplished, not by any occult, mysterious, or weird means, such as are employed by so-called mediums, but by scientific methods. If what we call personality exists after death, and that personality is anxious to communicate with those of us who are still in the flesh on this earth, there are two or three kinds of apparatus which should make communication very easy. I am engaged in the construction of one such apparatus now, and I hope to be able to finish it before very many months pass.

If those who have left the form of life that we have on earth cannot use, cannot move, the apparatus that I am going to give them the opportunity of moving, then the chance of there being a hereafter of the kind we think about and imagine goes down.

On the other hand, it will, of course, cause a tremendous sensation if it is successful.

I am working on the theory that our personality exists after what we call life leaves our present material bodies. If our personality dies, what's the use of a hereafter? What would it amount to? It wouldn't mean anything to us as individuals. If there is a hereafter which is to do us any good, we want our personality to survive, don't we?

If our personality survives, then it is strictly logical and scientific to assume that it retains memory, intellect, and other faculties and knowledge that we acquire on this earth. Therefore, if personality exists, after what we call death, it is reasonable to conclude that those who leave this earth would like to communicate with those they have left here. Accordingly, the thing to do is to furnish the best conceivable means to make it easy for them to open up communication with us, and then see what happens.

I am proceeding on the theory that in the very nature of things, the degree of material or physical power possessed by those in the next life must be extremely slight; and that, therefore, any instrument designed to be used to communicate with us must be super-delicate—as fine and responsive as human ingenuity can make it. For my part, I am inclined to believe that our personality hereafter will be able to affect matter. If this reasoning be correct, then, if we can evolve an instrument so delicate as to be affected, or moved, or manipulated—whichever term you want to use—by our personality as it survives in the next life, such an instrument, when made available, ought to record something.

I cannot believe for a moment that life in the first instance originated on this insignificant little ball which we call the earth—little, that is, in contrast with other bodies which inhabit space. The particles which combined to evolve living creatures on this planet of ours probably came from some other body elsewhere in the universe.

I don't believe for a moment that one life makes another life. Take our own bodies. I believe they are composed of myriads and myriads of infinitesimally small individuals, each in itself a unit of life, and that these units work in squads—or swarms, as I prefer to call them—and that these infinitesimally small units live forever. When we "die" these swarms of units, like a swarm of bees, so to speak, betake themselves elsewhere, and go on functioning in some other form or environment.

These life units are, of course, so infinitely small that probably a thousand of them aggregated together would not become visible under even the ultramicroscope, the most powerful magnifying instrument yet invented and constructed by man. These units, if they are as tiny as I believe them to be, would pass through a wall of stone or concrete almost as easily as they would pass through the air.

The more we learn the more we realize that there is life in things which we used to regard as inanimate, as lifeless. We now know that the difference between the lowest-known forms of animal life and trees or flowers or other plants is not so very great.

Small as these units of life are, they could still contain a sufficient number of ultimate particles of matter to form highly organized entities or individuals, with memory, certain varieties of skill, and other attributes of living entities. We, in our ignorance of all that pertains to life, have come to imagine that if certain things happen to a human being or an animal its whole life ceases. This notion has been repeatedly disproved in recent years.

The probability is that among units of life there are certain swarms which do most of the thinking and directing for other swarms. In other words, there are probably bosses, or leaders, among them, just as among humans. This theory would account for the fact that certain men and women have greater intellectuality, greater abilities, greater powers than others. It would account, too, for differences in moral character. One individual may be composed of a larger percentage of the higher order of these units of life than others. The moving out of myriads of what we may call the lower type of units of life and the influx of myriads of units of a higher order would explain the change which often takes place in the personality and character of individuals in the course of their existence on this earth.

The doctors long ago told us that our whole bodies undergo complete transformation every seven years, that no particle that entered into the composition of our bodies at the beginning of one seven-year period remains in our bodies at the end of seven years later. This means that matter is discarded, new matter being replaced by the working life-units or individuals. This rough-and-ready way of describing the discarding of defective matter that is constantly going on in our make-up would not be inconsistent with the theory I have evolved.

A common saying is, "We are creatures of environment." This is true, at least up to a certain point. We have seen how environment has wrought changes upon animals, and even wiped out certain species altogether—as the discovery of numerous skeletons of mammoth animals of prehistoric days has proved. Units of life, it is perfectly reasonable to deduce, require certain environment to function in certain ways, and when environment undergoes complete change, they seek other habitats, other dwellings, so to speak, for the carrying on of their functions.

Numerous experiments conducted by medical scientists have revealed that the memory is located in a certain section of the human brain called the fold of Broca. Now, to return to what is called "life after death." If the units of life which compose an individual's memory hold together after that individual's "death," is it not within range of possibility, to say the least, that these memory swarms could retain the powers they formerly possessed, and thus retain what we call the individual's personality after "dissolution" of the body? If so, then that individual's memory, or personality, ought to be able to function as before.

I am hopeful, therefore, that by providing the right kind of instrument, to be operated by this personality, we can receive intelligent messages from it in its changed habitation, or environment.

X-1920

XXXXIII · SPIRIT COMMUNICATION

I CANNOT conceive of such a thing as a spirit. Imagine something that has no weight, no material form, no mass; in a word, imagine nothing. I cannot be a party to the belief that spirits exist and can be seen under certain circumstances, and can be made to tilt tables and rap chairs and do other things of a similar and unimportant nature. The whole thing is so absurd.

I have been thinking for some time of a machine or apparatus which could be operated by personalities which have passed on to another existence or sphere. Now follow me carefully; I don't claim that our personalities pass on to another existence or sphere. I don't claim anything because I don't know anything about the subject. For that matter, no human being knows. But I do claim that it is possible to construct an apparatus which will be so delicate that if there are personalities in another existence or sphere who wish to get in touch with us in this existence or sphere, this apparatus will at least give them a better opportunity to express themselves than the tilting tables and raps and ouija boards and mediums and the other crude methods now purported to be the only means of communication.

In truth, it is the crudeness of the present methods that makes me doubt the authenticity of purported communications with deceased persons. Why should personalities in another existence or sphere waste their time working a little triangular piece of wood over a board with certain lettering on it? Why should such personalities play pranks with a table? The whole business seems so childish to me that I frankly cannot give it my serious consideration. I believe that if we are to make any real progress in psychic investigation, we must do it with scientific apparatus and in a scientific manner, just as we do in medicine, electricity, chemistry, and other fields.

Now what I propose to do is to furnish psychic investigators with an apparatus which will give a scientific aspect to their work. This apparatus, let me explain, is in the nature of a valve, so to speak. That is to say, the slightest conceivable effort is made to exert many times its initial power for indicative purposes. It is similar to a modern power house, where man, with his relatively puny one-eighth horse-power, turns a valve which starts a 50,000-horse-power steam turbine. My apparatus is along those lines, in that the slightest effort which it intercepts will be magnified many times so as to give us whatever form of record we desire for the purpose of investigation. Beyond that I don't care to say anything further regarding its nature. I have been working out the details for some time; indeed, a collaborator in this work died only the other day. In that he knew exactly what I am after in this work, I believe he ought to be the first to use it if he is able to do so. Of course, don't forget that I am making no claims for the survival of personality; I am not promising communication with those who have passed out of this life. I merely state that I am giving the psychic investigators an apparatus which may help them in their work, just as optical experts have given the miscroscope to the medical world. And if this apparatus fails to reveal anything of exceptional interest, I am afraid that I shall have lost all faith in the survival of personality as we know it in this existence.

I believe that life, like matter, is indestructible. There has always been a certain amount of life on this world and there will always be the same amount. You cannot create life; you cannot destroy life; you cannot multiply life.

The question has been raised that if these life entities are so small, they cannot be large enough to include a collection of organs capable of carrying on the tasks which I am about to mention. Yet why not? There is no limit to the smallness of things, just as there is no limit as to largeness. The electron theory gives us a reply which is wholly satisfactory. I have had the matter roughly calculated and have at hand the data of the calculation. I am sure that a highly organized entity, consisting of millions of electrons yet still remaining too small to be visible through any existing microscope, is possible.

There are many indications that we human beings act as a community or ensemble rather than as units. That is why I believe that each of us comprises millions upon millions of entities, and that our body and our mind represent the vote or the voice, whichever you wish to call it, of our entities.

Of course, you say, it is nature. But what is nature? That seems to me to be such an evasive reply. It means nothing. It is just a subterfuge—a convenient way of shutting off further questioning by merely giving an empty word for an answer. I have never been satisfied with that word "nature."

The entities are life, I again repeat. They are steady workers. In our bodies these entities constantly rebuild our tissues to replace those which are constantly wearing out. They watch after the functions of the various organs, just as the engineers in a power house see that the machinery is kept in perfect order. Once conditions become unsatisfactory in the body, either through a fatal sickness, fatal accident or old age, the entities simply depart from the body and leave little more than an empty structure behind. Being indefatigable workers, they naturally seek something else to do. They either enter into the body of another man, or even start work on some other form of life. At any rate, there is a fixed number of these entities, and it is the same entities that have served over and over again for everything in this universe of ours, although the various combinations of entities have given us an erroneous impression of new life and still new life for each generation.

The entities live forever. You cannot destroy them, just the same as you cannot destroy matter. You can change the form of matter; but of gold, iron, sulfur, oxygen and so on, there was the same quantity in existence in the beginning of this world as there is today. We are simply working the same supply over and over again. True, we change the combinations of these elements, but we have not changed the relative quantities of each of the elements with which we started. So with the life entities, we cannot destroy them. They are being used over and over again, in different forms, to be sure, but they are always the same entities.

The entities are so diversified in their capabilities that it is difficult to identify their handiwork in all instances. Thus today the scientists admit the difficulty of drawing a line of demarcation indicating where life ends and inanimate things begin. It may be that life entities even extend their work to minerals and chemicals. For what is it that causes certain solutions to form crystals of a very definite and intricate pattern? Nature! But what is nature? Is it not fair to even suspect that life entities may be at work building those crystals? They don't simply happen. Something must cause certain solutions always to form certain kinds of crystals.

Now we come to the matter of personality. The reason why you are you and I am Edison is because we have different swarms or groups or whatever you wish to call them, of entities. After eighty-two remarkable surgical operations the medical world has conclusively proved that the seat of our personality is in that part of the brain known as the fold of Broca. Now it is reasonable to suppose that the directing entities are located in that part of our bodies. These entities, as a closely-knit ensemble, give us our mental impressions and our personality.

I have already said that what we call death is simply the departure of the entities from our body. The whole question to my way of thinking, is what happens to the master entities—those located in the fold of Broca. It is fair to assume that the other entities, those which have been doing purely routine work in our body, disband and go off in various directions, seeking new work to do. But how about those which have been directing things in our body? Do they remain together as an ensemble or do they also break up and go about the universe seeking new tasks as individuals and not as a collective body? If they break up and set out as individual entities, then I very much fear that our personality does not survive. While the life entities live forever, thus giving us the eternal life which many of us hope for, this means little to you and me if, when we come to that stage known as death, our personality simply breaks up into separate units which soon combine with others to form new structures.

I do hope that our personality survives. If it does, then my apparatus ought to be of some use. That is why I am now at work on the most sensitive apparatus I have ever undertaken to build, and I await the results with the keenest interest.

X-30-1920

INDEX

Age, 57–58, 180–181
Aldrich, Thomas Bailey, 11
Atomic energy, 91–92
Automobiles, 109–111
Aviation, 91–93, 94–95, 98

Beethoven, Ludwig von, 82, 87
Boynsen, 11
Brontë, Charlotte, 7
Burroughs, John, 167–168

Cleveland, Miss, 19, 21, 22
Coeducation, 124
College, *see* Education
Composing, 87
Conservatism, 114
Crime, 113, 163–164

Darwin, Charles, 6, 228
Deafness, 44–55
Death, 179–180
De Quincy, Thomas, 7
De Vries theory, 228
Dickens, Charles, 7
Disarmament, 95–99, 201–202

Eastman, George, 75–76
Economic conditions, 96–97, 185–192, 199–202
  see also Gold Standard, Monetary conference
Education, 99–103, 107–114, 118–119, 123–125, 127–148, 163–164

Education—*cont'd*
  College, 127–128, 130–131, 133, 138–141
  Non-scholastic, 141–145
  Primary and Secondary, 130–131, 133–134
  see also Memory, Memory testing, Memory training, Musical education, Propaganda, Questionnaires, Tests, Thinking, Visual education
Einstein, Albert, 227
Energy, conservation of, 207–208
Environment, 231–232, 237–238
Evolution, 224–226, 228, 231

Fear, 185–187, 190, 192
Films, *see* Moving pictures, Talking pictures
Ford, Henry, 168–169

Gas, poison, 91, 94–95, 98
Gold standard, 192–200

Happiness, 58–59, 78, 162–163, 170, 171
Hawthorne, Nathaniel, 4–5
Heredity, 214–215, 222–223
Holzer, William, 5, 8–9
Howard, Governor, 17

Immortality, 205–206, 208–209, 217, 230, 234–235, 238, 241, 244

Incandescent light, 169
Individuality, 207, 216–222
Inventions, 179

Keller, Helen, 51–52
Kipling, Rudyard, 215
Kinetescope, 77–78

Labour, 94, 101, 103
Light, 51–52, 231–232

Macauley, Thomas Babington, 7
Machines, 165–166, 171–177
Mackaye, Steele, 7
Marriage, 143
Matter, conservation of, 206–208
Memory, 115–119, 129–130, 132, 136, 209–215
Memory testing, 114–117, 126
Memory training, 65–66, 68, 79
Monetary conference, 195–200
Montessori, 112
Morality, 121
Moving pictures, 63–79, 109, 112–113, 145–148, 164
see also Visual education
Music, 64, 79–88, 168, 169–170
America, 80–83, 87–88
Germany, 82, 87–88
see also Composing, Musical education, Musical instruments, Opera, Singing, Tests —Musical
Musical education, 81–83, 86–88
Musical instruments, 84–86
Muybridge, 72–74

Opera, 64, 83
Origin of life, 218, 222–224, 227–228, 235–237

Paine, Thomas, 151–158
Peace conferences, 91
see also Disarmament
Personality, 215, 230, 243–244
Phonograph, 50–51, 53–54, 55, 64, 70, 83–84, 85, 169–170
Porter, H. H., 7
Propaganda, 99–103

Questionnaires, 116, 118, 125–130, 132, 136–137, 139–140

Radicalism, 99–103
Radio, 50–51, 109, 143–145
Reading, 56–57
Reds, 101, 103
Reincarnation, 215
Religion, 36–37
Roche, John, 29
Roosevelt, Franklin D., 102–103
Roosevelt, Theodore, 157
Rossini, Gioacchino Antonio, 87
Russell, Lillian, 25

Selwyn, George, 4
Singing, 79–81, 83
Slavery, 172–173, 177
Sleep, 178
Smith, Sidney, 7, 26
Socialism, 164–165
Sound film, *see* Talking pictures
Spencer, Herbert, 162
Spiritualism, 205, 215–216, 224, 232–235, 238–241, 244
Stanford, Senator Leland, 72–73
Storage battery, 169
Strikes, 103
Subconscious mind, 132, 180, 221, 233
Submarines, 94

Takamini, 229
Talking pictures, 64–65
Tests, 115–117, 126–127, 129–130
    Musical, 83, 86–87
    Visual, 66–68
    see also Memory testing, Questionnaires
Thinking, 107, 113–114, 166–170
Travel, 109–111, 113

Unemployment, 187–190

Verdi, Giuseppe, 87

Visual education, 55, 63–68, 78–79, 112–114, 134, 137, 145–148, 164

Wagner, Richard, 87
War, 91–93, 94–98, 200–202
Winter, William, 7
World's Fair, 77, 108

Youth, 120–125, 127–128

Zoetrope, 72–73